PROPHECY AND COVENANT

STUDIES IN BIBLICAL THEOLOGY

A series of monographs designed to provide clergy and laymen with the best work in biblical scholarship both in this country and abroad.

Advisory Editors:

C. F. D. MOULE, *Lady Margaret's Professor of Divinity in the University of Cambridge*

JAMES BARR, *Professor of Semitic Languages and Literatures University of Manchester*

PETER ACKROYD, *Samuel Davidson Professor of Old Testament Studies University of London*

FLOYD V. FILSON, *Professor of New Testament Literature and History McCormick Theological Seminary, Chicago*

G. ERNEST WRIGHT, *Professor of Old Testament History and Theology at Harvard University*

STUDIES IN BIBLICAL THEOLOGY · 43

PROPHECY
AND COVENANT

R. E. CLEMENTS

SCM PRESS LTD
BLOOMSBURY STREET LONDON

SBN 334 01325 9
FIRST PUBLISHED 1965
SECOND IMPRESSION 1965
THIRD IMPRESSION 1968
© SCM PRESS LTD 1965
PRINTED IN GREAT BRITAIN
BY UNWIN BROTHERS LTD
WOKING AND LONDON

CONTENTS

PREFACE

A VERY prominent feature of the nineteenth-century attempts at a reconstruction of the ancient religion of Israel was the emphasis which they placed upon the creative contribution of the canonical prophets. The religion of Israel was regarded as a prophetic religion in the sense that its deepest insights and most creative achievements were thought to have been introduced through the preaching of the great prophets of the pre-exilic period. These men were claimed as the originators of a doctrine of ethical monotheism which has been of incalculable importance in the religious development of mankind. In consequence of this high estimate of the canonical prophets, they were separated quite sharply from the large numbers of other prophets whose activity is indirectly attested in the Old Testament, and inevitably a great deal of attention came to be given to the prophetic consciousness and to the psychology of prophetic inspiration.

Now much of this has changed with new methods of research and a more balanced appreciation of the significance of cult in ancient Israelite religion. Not least has there been a great change in the understanding of revelation itself in the Old Testament, with a shift away from an exaggerated emphasis upon its individual and psychological aspects. This monograph can make little claim to present a new approach to the prophets, or a new interpretation of them. Instead the aim has been to offer a comprehensive survey of many of the more recent studies of the prophetic writings which have been published. In particular the application of the techniques of form-criticism has opened up rich fields of enquiry into the background and character of the prophetic speeches, and their preservation in writing. Alongside of this, and vitally related to it, is a stronger emphasis upon the relationship of the prophets to the cult, and upon the significance of the cult as a medium of religious communication. The original home of prophecy was in the cult,

7

and both in form and substance the preaching of the prophets was greatly affected by the life and worship of Israel's great sanctuaries. Within the diversity of practice in Israel's worship, and underlying the varieties of prophetic utterance, I have believed it possible to discern some kind of unifying tendency. This was to be found in an overall concern with the covenant as the basis and explanation of Israel's existence. Why certain prophets differed from others, and preached a message which has ultimately been accorded canonical status, can only be finally explained by the attitude of such prophets to the covenant. Within the Old Testament we do not find a single source of revelation, either in the psychology of the prophetic consciousness, or in certain unique events, or in a single overall concept. Instead we find within Israel's religious traditions a tendency to become selective, and to establish certain normative patterns. There emerges what has been called the *canonical principle*. Ultimately the whole Old Testament came to be regarded as revelation, and to be invested with a canonical status. This short study endeavours to show how the preaching of certain prophets was held in a unique regard and became a formative influence in the development of the Israelite-Jewish religion, and in the production of the Old Testament.

The preparation of this book owes a great debt to the stimulus of Professor N. W. Porteous, who has himself published a number of articles which bear upon the theme of *Prophecy and Covenant*. Both to him and to Professor G. W. Anderson I also owe a debt of gratitude for the loan of books to which I should not otherwise have had access. Professor P. R. Ackroyd made a number of helpful criticisms and suggestions to the original manuscript, as also did Professor James Barr and Dr William McKane. To all these scholars I am indebted for the interest and advice which they have offered. Thanks are also due to the SCM Press for their kindness in accepting this monograph for the series *Studies in Biblical Theology*.

R. E. CLEMENTS

ABBREVIATIONS

AO	*Acta Orientalia*
ARW	*Archiv für Religionswissenschaft*
ATANT	Abhandlungen zur Theologie des Alten und Neuen Testaments
ATD	Das Alte Testament Deutsch
BA	*The Biblical Archaeologist*
BJRL	*Bulletin of the John Rylands Library*
BKAT	Biblischer Kommentar. Altes Testament
BSAW	*Berichte über die Verhandlungen der sächsischen Akademie der Wissenschaften zu Leipzig*
BWANT	Beiträge zur Wissenschaft vom Alten und Neuen Testament
BZAW	Beihefte zur Zeitschrift für die alttestamentliche Wissenschaft
CT	Cahiers théologiques
ExpT	*Expository Times*
EvTh	*Evangelische Theologie*
EVV	English Versions
FRLANT	Forschungen zur Religion und Literatur des Alten und Neuen Testaments
HAT	Handbuch zum Alten Testament
HUCA	*Hebrew Union College Annual*
IDB	*The Interpreter's Dictionary of the Bible*
JAOS	*Journal of the American Oriental Society*
JBL	*Journal of Biblical Literature*
JNES	*Journal of Near Eastern Studies*
JSS	*Journal of Semitic Studies*
JTS	*Journal of Theological Studies*
MUSJ	*Mélanges de l'université Saint Joseph, Beyrouth*
OTS	Oudtestamentische Studiën
RGG	*Die Religion in Geschichte und Gegenwart*

Abbreviations

RHPR	*Revue d'histoire et de philosophie religieuses*
RSV	Revised Standard Version
SANT	Studien zum Alten und Neuen Testament
SBT	Studies in Biblical Theology
SEA	*Svensk exegetisk årsbok*
StTh	*Studia theologica*
SVT	Supplements to Vetus Testamentum
TGUOS	*Transactions of the Glasgow University Oriental Society*
TLZ	*Theologische Literaturzeitung*
TS	Theologische Studien
TZ	*Theologische Zeitschrift*
UUA	Uppsala Universitets årsskrift
VT	*Vetus Testamentum*
WMANT	Wissenschaftliche Monographien zum Alten und Neuen Testament
ZAW	*Zeitschrift für die alttestamentliche Wissenschaft*
ZEE	*Zeitschrift für evangelische Ethik*
ZTK	*Zeitschrift für Theologie und Kirche*

I

PROPHECY AND THE PROPHETS

THE modern study of the Old Testament, in its manifold tasks of uncovering the origin, nature and theological significance of the documents which make up the first part of the Christian Bible, must continually address itself to the quest to recover the form and content of the religion of Ancient Israel. It is out of this religion that the Old Testament grew, and it is only by obtaining a clear understanding of what this religion meant for all who participated in its worship, and who shared its beliefs and hopes, that we can ourselves hope to discern the enduring importance of the Old Testament for the Jewish and Christian faiths. Yet in our quest to uncover the early religion of Israel it is apparent even to the cursory reader of the Old Testament that this literature presents a very distinctive view of that religion, and that at many points instead of describing the contemporary faith and practice, it roundly condemns it. The religion of Ancient Israel gave birth to the Old Testament and jealously guarded it, yet in doing so, it preserved what was very often its own most severe critic. The religion of the Old Testament, if we may so term the ideas which this literature contains, is not co-terminous with the religion of Ancient Israel, which was both older and broader in its manifestations.[1] Nevertheless the two are vitally interrelated, and without a clear grasp of the essential nature of Israelite religion, the distinctive contribution and character of the Old Testament will be lost to us. A theology of the Old Testament cannot be indifferent to a careful and exact appreciation of the actual religion of Ancient Israel as it once existed in a historical community. It is therefore a work of primary theological importance to examine the origin of the Old Testament in its setting in the religion of Ancient Israel, and to discover why this literature arose, and why its own dis-

[1] Cf. on this point the remarks of T. C. Vriezen, *An Outline of Old Testament Theology*, Oxford, 1958, pp. 121ff.

tinctive attitude to its contemporary religious background was felt to be worthy of preservation.

In this regard it is immediately apparent from the nature of our sources that the Old Testament occupies a unique position in our knowledge of the ancient near-eastern world. What we can discover today of the religions of Ancient Egypt and Mesopotamia, or for that matter, of Canaan, is largely a consequence of the chance preservation of literary and inscriptional remains, illuminated and enriched by the religious architecture and artefacts that the archaeologist has uncovered. The evidence that is left for us to examine is very much the fortuitous result of geographical, historical and cultural circumstances; the kind of building materials in use, the prevailing weather and, not least, the vicissitudes of war, have all combined to preserve some of the evidence and to destroy much that is important. In the Old Testament, however, we have a very different situation, since this literature was consciously preserved by pious men, who did so because they considered it a part of their religious obligation. The Old Testament canon did not come into existence by chance, but by a conscious and sustained concern on the part of Israelites and Jews, who, over a period of many centuries, cherished certain traditions about themselves and their religion. To know why they did so is a study which greatly deepens our understanding of the Old Testament itself. When ultimately this literature was accorded canonical status by Jews and Christians, it was not to invest it with a new authority, but to accord to it a status commensurate with the authority which they sensed it already held for themselves. It was no arbitrary decision, but simply a formal recognition of what had long been a commonly accepted fact. Only in certain minor cases was there any room for doubt or disputation, since the main lines of the canon had already taken on a firm shape. The very existence of the Old Testament therefore is a theological fact of great significance, and to investigate the origins of this literature in its historical basis in the religion of Ancient Israel is a very worth while undertaking. If we would understand the theological meaning of the Old Testament we must continually relate it to the historical religion of Israel in which it arose, and seek to discover the purpose which occasioned its preservation. It soon becomes clear that this purpose was not simply to provide a descriptive account of what that religion was, but to establish a witness as to what that religion should have been. The Old Testament continually transcends the contemporary religion of Israel, for, whilst it arose out of it, it points to a purity of faith, and a standard of morality, which that religion as a whole never attained. We cannot understand the Old Testament therefore without paying attention to this normative function which it seeks to fulfil. It is a series of writings which arose out of a religion, and long after that religion ceased to be practised in its original historical form, these writings have maintained their importance for the daughter faiths of Judaism and Christianity. Neither of these faiths can identify itself wholly with the ancient religion of Israel, although they derive much from it, yet they both find in the Old Testament a book which speaks to them about their God.

This phenomenon, of the production of a literature out of a religious situation which has endured long after the original situation has passed away, presents itself to us most forcibly in the books of the prophets. Here we have, quite clearly, the recorded account of the preaching and activity of certain prophets in the Old Testament, chosen out of a much older and more widespread experience of prophetic preaching and inspiration. Why did these prophets differ from others, and why did they become canonical? The mere claim to a special kind of inspiration cannot explain this, since the other prophets also claimed a like inspiration. Nor can the answer be found in arguing that the canonical prophets were conscious of a different method, or technique, of inspiration, since there is no adequate evidence to prove such to have been the case.[1] On the contrary these persons, in endeavouring to convince their hearers of the truth of their preaching, knew that they possessed no outward sign or proof for their claim, but were dependent

[1] S. Mowinckel ('The "Spirit" and the "Word" in the Pre-exilic Reforming Prophets', *JBL* 53, 1934, pp. 199ff.; postscript, *JBL* 56, 1937, pp. 261ff.) attempted to distinguish between the inspiration by possession of the spirit in the ordinary prophets, and the special inspiration of the word in the canonical prophets. This, however, cannot be maintained. See H. H. Rowley, 'The Nature of Prophecy in the Light of Recent Study', *The Servant of the Lord*, London, 1954, pp. 111ff.; cf. *The Rediscovery of the Old Testament*, London, 1945, pp. 98f. No psychological or institutional distinction can be made the yardstick of evaluation between the canonical prophets and the other prophets. Cf. A. H. J. Gunneweg, *Mündliche und schriftliche Tradition der vorexilischen Prophetenbücher als Problem der neueren Prophetenforschung* (FRLANT 73), Göttingen, 1959, pp. 91ff.

solely upon God to vindicate it. They appealed to the consciences of Israel, and they pointed to historical events as the final proof that their message was true. Their distinctiveness, therefore, lies in the particular message which they gave, not in the form in which it was delivered, and the permanent recording and preservation of their preaching was a consequence of the specific import and intrinsic significance which that message was felt to possess.[1] This significance was not because they preached new doctrines in the spheres of morality and theology, since the canonical prophets did not regard themselves as first and foremost innovators in their teaching on these subjects. It must rather be found in their attitude to Israel itself, and to the covenant with Yahweh, which was the basis of its life.

The fact that the work of the canonical prophets arose out of the activity of a much larger prophetic movement in Israel throws up in a particularly clear form the question of the relation of the Old Testament to the religion of Ancient Israel. It is no accident therefore that the interpretation of the prophets, and their place in the religion of Israel, is a question which has come very much to the fore in modern study of the problems concerning Old Testament theology. We must ask ourselves afresh, What place are we to give to prophecy in a theology of the Old Testament? Is it a phenomenon that must be treated by itself, or can we subsume it under some other heading such as the covenant, or the election traditions?

We are today, in our study of the Old Testament, in a far better position to understand the prophets in their contemporary historical setting than was possible a generation ago, when the religious history of Israel was less adequately understood. This is not to deny that there are still enormous gaps in our knowledge, and an immense amount of research remains to be done, but we may claim that the results of a fresh study of the literature, with new techniques of criticism, and a more balanced understanding of the

[1] Cf. S. Mowinckel, 'Literature', *IDB* III, p. 142a, who points out that only Israel's prophets gave rise to a literature of world importance, a fact which he ascribes jointly to the spiritual originality of the prophets, and the uniqueness of the religion of Israel. I. Engell, *The Call of Isaiah. An Exegetical and Comparative Study* (UUA, 1949:4), Uppsala, 1949, p. 60, ascribes the preservation of the prophetic books to 'the Yahwistic tendency, especially in its positive-messianic aspect'.

contribution of the cult, have enabled us to avoid the one-sidedness which marred the earlier study of the prophets. The great contributions to our understanding of the Old Testament made by J. Wellhausen and B. Duhm, and their many followers, did the prophets a disservice by claiming too much for them.[1] By regarding the prophets as the greatest products of Israel's religion, and, more significantly, as its real creators, they raised prophecy out of its context in the religious tradition of Israel. By claiming the canonical prophets as the first teachers of ethical monotheism, and by tracing the gradual unfolding of such a doctrine of God in the succession of the prophets, a false picture of them was created which made them theologians rather than Yahweh's messengers.[2]

When this understanding of prophecy was integrated with the study of the other literature of the Old Testament, it was inevitable that the influence of the prophets was thought to be perceptible in most of its writings. Thus the Psalms and the Wisdom writings were thought to betray such a prophetic influence. The whole was a neat, historically credible and schematic view of the history and development of the religion of Ancient Israel. A consequence of this view, and the high place it accorded to the prophets as the true pioneers of faith in Israel, was that the attention of scholars was directed mainly towards the ethical and theological ideas expressed by the prophets, and eventually to the psychology of prophetic inspiration itself.[3] It was here that their distinctiveness

---

[1] Cf. B. Duhm, *Israels Propheten*, Tübingen, 1916, p. 8: 'Prophecy is not simply a remarkable phenomenon, but means the beginning of the spiritual history of the world, and has had a greater influence on it than the philosophers of Greece, or the wise men of India. . . . The period which followed the two centuries of the flowering of prophecy represents a decline.' For recent exaggerated claims for the prophetic influence on the Old Testament see C. F. Whitley, *The Prophetic Achievement*, London, 1963, and J. Jocz, *The Spiritual History of Israel*, London, 1961.

[2] Cf. J. Wellhausen, 'Israel' (rep. from *Encyclopaedia Brittanica*), *Prolegomena to the History of Israel*, Edinburgh, 1885, p. 474, for the claim that the prophets were the first ethical monotheists. For a more recent presentation see C. F. Whitley, *op. cit.*, pp. 93ff.

[3] The question of the psychology of prophetic inspiration arose most especially since the major study of G. Hölscher, *Die Propheten. Untersuchungen zur Religionsgeschichte Israels*, Leipzig, 1914, pp. 1ff. Hölscher stressed the ecstatic nature of prophecy, on which see more recently J. Lindblom, *Prophecy in Ancient Israel*, Oxford, 1962, pp. 47ff., 197ff., 299ff., and F. Maass, 'Zur psychologischen Sonderung der Ekstase', *Wissenschaftliche Zeitschrift*, *Leipzig*, Gesellschaft und sprachwissenschaftliche Reihe 3, 1953-4, pp. 297ff.

was thought to be found. Their theological and moral ideas are no doubt important, but it is untrue to the prophets themselves to lift these out of their setting, and to regard them as the main factor in their preaching.

In the first place the prophets did not regard themselves as introducing a new doctrine of God in Israel, or as teaching a new morality. On the contrary their ethical teaching appears incidentally in their condemnation of the people for unrighteous and immoral behaviour, and the prophets clearly expected their hearers to know what they were talking about. Their accusations would have been false had the people not already known the ethical standards which Yahweh demanded. The prophets accuse them of failing to keep what they had long known to be the will of Yahweh. Similarly in the realm of theological ideas, the prophets assert that Yahweh is the God of Israel, and although each of them had his own distinctive emphasis, they did not try to teach a doctrine of Yahweh that was markedly new in Israel. Rather it is the people who are said to have rejected the true knowledge of God in preferring their own innovations, and the prophets claim that they are speaking in the name of Yahweh who had long ago revealed himself to Israel. The prophets were the heirs of a very rich and full tradition, which was certainly not devoid of theological insight and moral value.[1] Although in the society around them this religious tradition had suffered a considerable breakdown and decay, yet its existence cannot be doubted. The central focus of such a tradition was the belief in a covenant between Yahweh and Israel, with its double themes of the divine grace revealed in Israel's election, and the divine demand proclaimed in the covenant law.

The central concern of the prophetic preaching was with Yahweh's relationship to Israel, and his dealings with them in the arena of history. It is true that the oracles against foreign nations are a large and important part of the prophetic corpus, yet the first interest of the prophets is in God's action towards Israel, and sometimes even the oracles against foreign nations have an indirect

[1] Cf. N. W. Porteous, 'The Religion of Israel: Prophecy', *Record and Revelation,* ed. H. W. Robinson, Oxford, 1938, p. 217; E. Würthwein, 'Der Ursprung der prophetischen Gerichtsrede', *ZTK* 49, 1952, pp. 1ff.; S. Mowinckel, *Die Erkenntnis Gottes bei den alttestamentlichen Profeten,* Oslo, 1941, pp. 9ff., 32; G. von Rad, *Theologie des A.T.* II, Munich, 1960, *passim.*

concern with Israel. It is because of what they had to say about the relationship between Yahweh and his people that these prophets were heard to say something new, and of vital significance for Israel itself. Thus eventually their words were recorded and preserved because they were known to be sayings of enduring importance for the life and hope of the people of God. What they had to say in the realms of morality and theology was an integral part of what they had to say about God's encounter with his people. The canonical prophets are thus very much concerned with Israel as the covenant people of Yahweh, and consequently with the covenant by which Israel's life was governed.

From the evidence of the prophets themselves therefore we must reject an evaluation which makes them into great religious individualists, independent of the established forms of religion, and of any, save a few, predecessors.[1] The prophets were vitally connected and concerned with the traditional forms of religion in Israel, even though they were compelled at several points to condemn its contemporary manifestations. Besides this, however, recent study of the Psalter and of the Wisdom literature shows that we cannot regard all occurrences of lofty religious and ethical ideas in Israel as dependent on the classical prophets. Rather we must see prophecy, religious poetry and song, as well as Wisdom teaching, as parallel forms of spiritual and literary activity. At many points they intersect and borrow, the one from the other, and all together go back to something prior to them all as the essential presupposition of their message. This is in the covenant tradition of Israel, rooted in the conviction of Yahweh's intervention to rescue some Hebrew slaves out of Egypt, and of the covenant-making on Mount Sinai, in which Yahweh revealed the basis of law which was to form the moral foundation of Israel's life. Only in the early Wisdom teaching, as a result of its own

[1] We may contrast the evaluation of J. Wellhausen, which was an essential presupposition of his estimate of prophecy, 'It belongs to the notion of prophecy, of true revelation, that Jehovah, overlooking all the media of ordinances and institutions, communicates Himself to the *individual*, the called one, in whom that mysterious and irreducible rapport in which the deity stands with man clothes itself with energy. Apart from the prophet, in abstracto, there is no revelation; it lives in his divine-human ego', *Prolegomena to the History of Israel*, p. 398. Cf. also C. F. Whitley, *op. cit.*, pp. 24ff., for the claim that, 'The great creative prophets were but little indebted to traditional Israelite belief for the content of their message' (p. 43).

particular interests and style, is the covenant tradition noticeably absent. This is particularly true of the oldest phase of the development of Israelite Wisdom, which reflected the empirical and international outlook of its near-eastern origins. Yet as the pursuit of Wisdom progressed in Israel it became increasingly influenced, and ultimately circumscribed, by the tradition of the covenant and its law.[1]

For the prophets and the psalmists the covenant tradition formed the heart of their religion, and for the Wisdom teachers it became an indispensable presupposition.

The importance of the covenant basis of Israel's faith and life has become very much more apparent in recent research into its origins as a people. Most especially the work of M. Noth has shown that the earliest organization of Israel we can trace shows it to have been a federation of tribes, who were united by their covenant relationship to Yahweh.[2] For theology the fact of this covenant basis of Israel is more important than the subordinate questions of the number of tribes originally involved in the federation and the locality of its formation. The importance of this covenant concept for Old Testament studies must not be underrated, and it may not be out of place to stress at this point that the recognition of the basis of Israel's life in a covenant with Yahweh is the result of historical research into Israel's origins, not the consequence of a theological methodology applied to the Old Testament.

[1] Cf. J. C. Rylaarsdam, *Revelation in Jewish Wisdom Literature*, Chicago, 1946. Rylaarsdam points out that the earliest Wisdom teaching made no use of the national religious tradition, but in course of time it was touched by its spirit and shared its practices; from conceiving originally of revelation wholly in natural terms, it came ultimately to regard it wholy as a gift of God: *op. cit.*, especially pp. 23, 72f. Cf. also G. von Rad, *Old Testament Theology* I, Edinburgh, 1962, pp. 418ff., 445.

[2] M. Noth, *Das System der Zwölf Stämme Israels* (BWANT IV:1), Stuttgart, 1930, *passim*; *A History of Israel* (2nd Eng. ed.), London, 1960, pp. 85ff. Cf. also W. Beyerlin, *Herkunft und Geschichte der ältesten Sinaitraditionen*, Tübingen, 1961, pp. 165ff.; G. E. Mendenhall, 'Covenant', *IDB* I, pp. 718ff. Recently R. Smend, *Jahwekreig und Stämmebund* (FRLANT 84), Göttingen, 1963, *passim*, has endeavoured to show that the institution of the holy war formed an older and more fundamental factor in the growth of Israel, than did the amphictyonic covenant. Cf. also his *Die Bundesformel* (TS 68), Zürich, 1963, pp. 14ff. Important criticisms, on historical grounds, of Noth's presentation of the Israelite amphictyony are made by S. Herrmann, 'Das Werden Israels', *TLZ* 87, 1962, cols. 561ff.

Alongside of this awareness that the covenant was basic to Israel's earliest life and faith has come a more positive appreciation of the cult as a vehicle of religious communication. In particular it is apparent that the earliest recollection and reaffirmation of the covenant in Israel took place in a cultic assembly.[1] The tribes renewed their pledge of allegiance to the covenant and its obligations at the central sanctuary accepted by the tribes. This celebration of the making of the covenant, with a renewal on the part of the tribes of their oath of loyalty to each other and to Yahweh, took place in the autumn, and this gave to Israel a religious celebration of the utmost importance. Amongst the peoples who surrounded Israel, and who influenced its development, this Autumn Festival had a special significance as a New Year celebration, but in Israel it took on the character of a covenant festival, which recalled and renewed the original establishing of the covenant.[2]

The clearer perception of the origin of the Psalter in Israel's cult, together with the realization of the antiquity of many psalms, forbids that we should ignore the cult as of little spiritual significance. It was the cult, and not the canonical prophets, which provided the forms and ideas which moulded Hebrew psalmody. At many points it was the prophets who borrowed from the language and style of the cult-hymns, not the psalmists who borrowed from the prophets. The close relationship of many of

[1] M. Noth, *Das System der Zwölf Stämme Israels*, pp. 66ff., where Noth connects such a covenant celebration with the assembly at Shechem, mentioned in Josh. 24. The importance of this covenant festival for the development of Israel's cult, psalmography and historical traditions is emphasized by A. Weiser, *The Psalms*, London, 1962, pp. 26ff., and frequently. Cf. also his *Introduction to the Old Testament*, London, 1961, pp. 83ff., and 'Zur Frage nach den Beziehungen der Psalmen zum Kult; die Darstellung der Theophanie in den Psalmen und in Festkult', *Glaube und Geschichte im A.T.*, Munich, 1961, pp. 303ff.

[2] The importance of the Autumn Festival as a covenant celebration is fundamental to A. Weiser's understanding of the cult, and to his interpretation of the Psalms. Whilst we do not share all of Weiser's views on the connexion of so many psalms with this feast, the importance of recognizing the distinctive Israelite character of the Autumn Festival as a covenant feast cannot be overlooked. This is now admitted by S. Mowinckel, *The Psalms in Israel's Worship*, Oxford, 1962, I, pp. 136ff., 155, where he corrects the emphasis of his earlier views expressed in *Psalmenstudien* II: *Das Thronbesteigungsfest Jahwäs und der Ursprung der Eschatologie*, rep. Amsterdam, 1961, pp. 1ff.

the Old Testament psalms with other near-eastern poetry and cult-hymns, both as regards form and, in part also, language, has greatly strengthened the arguments for the early origins of Israelite psalmody. It can now be confidently claimed that at least from the time when the temple was built in Jerusalem under Solomon, Israel developed a rich tradition of cult-hymnography, in which an initial influence from the Canaanites was not unimportant. The present Old Testament Psalter was produced over a long period out of collections of such cult-hymns, by a constant process of revision and addition. From these psalms we gain an insight into the early religion of Israel which shows it to have been both elevated, and far from lacking in moral content. This religion, to which the Psalter testifies, must be regarded as the background of the great prophets, rather than as a consequence of their preaching.[1]

The Jerusalem cult in particular, with its own distinctive heritage, placed a quite exceptional emphasis upon the cosmic and supra-national power of Yahweh, as the King of the universe. Even though this did not wholly amount to monotheism, with the complete repudiation of the existence of other gods, it certainly did not rank any other divine being alongside Yahweh, nor regard Yahweh's activity and interest as limited to Israel. The full-grown monotheistic preaching of Deutero-Isaiah appears to be more dependent upon the ideas and language of the pre-exilic cult at Jerusalem, than upon any specific prophetic predecessor.

Even to present the situation in this way, however, is to over-simplify it, since we cannot any longer rest content with the notion that the cultic circles of Israel and the prophetic circles were wholly separate and unrelated groups.[2] From the earliest days of Israel's worship we are led to see that prophets appeared and delivered their oracles in close association with the sanc-

[1] Cf. S. Mowinckel, 'Literature', *IDB* III, p. 142: 'The religion of the Psalms is the spiritual background of the prophets, who always stood in close connection with the temple and the cult.'

[2] For the relationship between the prophetic and priestly circles in Israel see A. C. Welch, *Prophet and Priest in Old Israel*, rep. Oxford, 1953; N. W. Porteous, 'Living Issues in Biblical Scholarship: Prophet and Priest in Israel', *ExpT* 62, 1950–51, pp. 4ff.; O. Plöger, 'Priester und Prophet', *ZAW* 63, 1951, pp. 157ff.

tuaries.[1] Many of them were in permanent association with the shrines, and were regarded as established functionaries of the cult. They delivered oracles for the benefit of those who visited the shrine, and they had a particular part to play in the rites that took place. As members of the larger staff of the great temple of Jerusalem, and also no doubt of the great shrines of North Israel at Bethel and Dan, such cultic prophets had a specific function to fulfil. In these situations they developed patterns of oracular utterance, and established accepted modes of address, which formed a basis of speech-forms which the canonical prophets inherited. The work of such cultic prophets is to be found at more than one point in the Psalter. Some psalms were certainly composed by these prophetic temple personnel, and in the liturgical celebrations at which the psalms were used, it often fell to these prophets to answer in the name of Yahweh the requests and entreaties of his worshippers. The oracular form which is sometimes encountered in the Psalms is a direct consequence of this prophetic activity. The relationship between psalmody and prophetic utterance was one of mutual influence, not a one-sided dependence of the psalmists on the prophets. As a consequence of this new appreciation of the relationship of prophecy to the cult, it is clear that we cannot dismiss the attitude of the canonical prophets to the priesthood and sanctuaries as a rejection motivated by an institutional opposition. In a number of ways the prophets were dependent on the cult so that their condemnation of cultic activity and officials will appear in a new light, simply because this condemnation itself was a very remarkable feature of the canonical prophets over against the attitude of their predecessors. That we are able to appreciate more adequately the spiritual presuppositions and aims of the cult means that we can enquire more intelligently after the reasons for the prophetic hostility to its contemporary manifestation.

[1] Cf. S. Mowinckel, *Psalmenstudien* III: *Kultprophetie und prophetische Psalmen,* rep. Amsterdam, 1961, *passim,* and *The Psalms in Israel's Worship* II, pp. 53ff.; H. Junker, *Prophet und Seher in Israel,* Trier, 1927, pp. 22ff.; A. R. Johnson, 'The Prophet in Israelite Worship', *ExpT* 47, 1935–6, pp. 312ff., and *The Cultic Prophet in Ancient Israel* (2nd ed.), Cardiff, 1962. See also A. Haldar, *Associations of Cult Prophets among the Ancient Semites,* Uppsala, 1945, which suffers from a lack of attention to the distinctive elements of Israelite prophecy. A critical and sceptical attitude to the theory of cult-prophets is shown by G. Quell, 'Der Kultprophet', *TLZ* 81, 1956, cols. 401ff.

In relation to the Wisdom teachers and their activity we can no longer maintain that these also were dependent on the ethical teaching of the prophets. From the days of Solomon's introduction of a Wisdom school in Jerusalem the interest and literary styles of the wise men, with their international outlook, began to exert some influence on Israelite literature.[1] Both psalmody and prophecy owe a debt to this,[2] and they in their turn exerted a reciprocal influence on the wise men. In Israel the presupposition of the covenantal basis of the nation's life set certain limits to the range of Wisdom speculations and teaching, and the prophetic attitude to the covenant eventually lent a more nationalistic flavour to Israelite Wisdom.

Another factor necessitating the reappraisal of the place of the prophets in Israel's religious development is occasioned by the recent study of the place of law in Ancient Israel. In Wellhausen's reconstruction of Israel's religious development the ethical content of the law was regarded as essentially dependent on the prophets.[3] The pre-exilic religion of Israel was believed to have been the age of the great classical prophets, and to have provided the really creative period of Israel's life. After the exile the returning community endeavoured to live according to the ethical teaching of the prophets by systematizing that teaching in the form of law. Thus Judaism arose as an adherance to a law, which eventually became legalistic and formal. The first step in this direction was claimed to have been occasioned by the Josianic reform (621 BC), in which the central corpus of Deuteronomic law, based on the ethical teaching of the eighth-century prophets, was made the official rule of Israel's life. With this, Israel became the people of a book. The post-exilic prophets, beginning in the

---

[1] For the Solomonic origin of Wisdom in Israel, and its particular character, see A. Alt, 'Die Weisheit Salomos', *Kleine Schriften* II, Munich, 1953, pp. 90ff. R. B. Y. Scott, 'Solomon and the Beginnings of Wisdom in Israel', *Wisdom in Israel and in the Ancient Near East: Presented to H. H. Rowley* . . . (SVT 3), Leiden, 1955, pp. 262ff., is very sceptical of a Solomonic origin for Israelite Wisdom, and connects it rather with the age of Hezekiah.

[2] Cf. J. Lindblom, 'Wisdom in the Old Testament Prophets', *Wisdom in Israel* (SVT 3), pp. 192ff.; S. Mowinckel, 'Psalms and Wisdom', *ibid.*, pp. 205ff.; S. Terrien, 'Amos and Wisdom', *Israel's Prophetic Heritage*, ed. B. W. Anderson and W. Harrelson, London, 1962, pp. 108ff.; J. Fichtner, 'Jesaja unter den Weisen', *TLZ* 74, 1949, cols. 75ff.

[3] Cf. J. Wellhausen, *Prolegomena to the History of Israel*, pp. 399ff., 420ff.

exile with Ezekiel, were thought to represent a declining insight into the spiritual nature of religion, when compared to their predecessors. They fostered the spirit of Judaism by their concern with the cult, and with the exact performance of certain moral and ritual obligations. The highest achievements of Israelite law, particularly in the Decalogue (Ex. 20.2–17), and the Book of Deuteronomy, with its demand of love for Yahweh, were claimed to be dependent on the teaching of the great prophets.

The form-critical and traditio-historical investigations into the nature and origins of Israelite law have rendered such a view untenable. Researches in this field have shown that a basis of law goes back to the very earliest stage of Israel's existence as a covenant community.[1] Whatever date we accord to the extant Ethical Decalogue it is certain that the institution and use of such a foundation of law, declared to the gathered assembly of Israel's representatives, is of very ancient usage, and belongs to the essential nature of the covenant. From the beginnings of the covenant of Israel a foundation of law, most probably in decalogic form, was used to establish a standard of conduct among the people. We must therefore recognize that a basis of law, with a strongly moral tone, was anterior to the prophets, rather than owing its origin to a dependence on them. The institution of a tradition of law, with both ethical and cultic regulations, was indigenous to Israel's cult, and forms a permanent feature of the covenant relationship between Yahweh and Israel. It is to this tradition of a covenantal code of conduct that the great prophets of the eighth and seventh centuries appealed when they accused their nation of disloyalty to Yahweh, and of disregard of his revealed demands.

The picture that now presents itself to us of Israel's religious development is not that of a successive elaboration of the religious insights obtained by the great prophets of the eighth and seventh centuries, but of a series of traditions proceeding and developing side by side. Law, psalmography, Wisdom and prophecy all had their own distinctive place, and maintained their own particular

---

[1] Cf. A. Alt, 'Die Ursprünge des israelitischen Rechts', *Kleine Schriften* I, pp. 328ff.; M. Noth, 'Die Gesetze im Pentateuch. Ihre vorraussetzungen und ihr Sinn', *Ges. Stud.z.A.T.* (2 Aufl.), Munich, 1960, pp. 32ff.; G. E. Mendenhall, 'Ancient Oriental and Biblical Law', *BA* 17, 1954, pp. 26ff.

traditions. Each of these traditions was able to work with a basis of inherited forms and ideas which Israel took over from Canaan, or brought with it into the land, whilst the controlling factor in the development of each of them was Israel's knowledge of its covenant relationship to Yahweh. At innumerable places the lines of tradition intersect. Law and prophecy proceeded together in Israel's life, and although the classical prophets could appeal to a tradition of law already in existence, they were not themselves without influence upon the recognition and development of that law. The same is true also of the Wisdom schools and of the development of psalmography in the cult, which were not unaffected by the rise of the great prophets.

The application of form-criticism to the prophetic writings has illuminated in a striking fashion the role of the prophet as Yahweh's messenger.[1] The characteristic prophetic opening of an oracle with, 'Thus says Yahweh . . .', and the frequent conclusion, '. . . oracle (Heb. *nĕ'um*) of Yahweh', have their origin in the speech forms used by a messenger carrying out the commission of his master.[2] This particular stylistic device, which is so fundamental to the prophetic speech, delineates the role of the prophets as the bearers of a message from their divine Lord. Just as the messenger's significance did not lie in himself, but in the message which he brought, so the prophet's person was subordinate to the message which he was commissioned to deliver. Yet it was inevitable that attention should have been attracted to the

---

[1] Cf. especially L. Köhler, *Deuterojesaja (Jesaja 40–55) stilkritisch untersucht* (BZAW 37), Giessen, 1923, pp. 102ff.; H. Wildberger, *Jahwewort und prophetische Rede bei Jeremia*, Zürich, 1942, pp. 48ff.; C. Westermann, *Grundformen prophetischer Rede*, Munich, 1960, esp. pp. 7off.; R. Rendtorff, 'Prophetenspruch' *RGG*³ V, cols. 635–8, and 'Botenformel und Botenspruch', *ZAW* 74, 1962, pp. 165ff.; J. F. Ross, 'The Prophet as Yahweh's Messenger', *Israel's Prophetic Heritage*, ed. Anderson and Harrelson, pp. 98ff.

[2] On the use of these formulae see R. Rendtorff, 'Zum Gebrauch der Formel *nĕ'um Jahwe* im Jeremiabuch', *ZAW* 66, 1954, pp. 27ff.; F. Baumgärtel, 'Zu den Gottesnamen in den Büchern Jeremia und Ezechiel', *Verbannung und Heimkehr*, ed. A. Kuschke, Tübingen, 1961, pp. 20ff., and 'Die Formel *nĕ'um Jahwe*', *ZAW* 73, 1961, pp. 277ff. Baumgärtel seeks to establish that 'Thus says Yahweh . . .' originated as an oracle formula associated with the ark, whilst 'oracle of Yahweh' originated with the older *nĕbhi'im* (cf. Balaam in Num. 24.3f., 15f.), and was characteristic for divinatory prophecy. It is impossible, however, to derive such general terms from such specific situations, and the probability is much rather that speech-forms used by a messenger were adopted quite early by prophets for the delivery of their oracles.

figure of the prophet as a man who stood in a unique relationship to God, and who was endowed with exceptional divine gifts. This is already apparent in the early period by the description of a prophet as a 'man of God' (Heb. *'īsh 'ĕlōhīm*), a title which is peculiar to prophets. It is further evidenced by the remarkable collection of traditions which centred around Elijah and Elisha. In the case of Elisha in particular more attention is given to the prophet as a man possessed of outstanding powers than to any message which he uttered. It is apparent therefore that even in the period before Amos the special gifts of the prophet tended to isolate him from other men, and to invest him with a unique status as a man full of God's spirit. Among the classical prophets we find that the experiences and sufferings of Jeremiah entered deeply into the whole significance of his prophetic ministry and message.[1] Both historical and temperamental factors were undoubtedly responsible for this involvement of the prophet's personality in his word.

From this brief survey we can discern that the understanding of the relationship of the canonical prophets to other religious institutions in Ancient Israel, the cult, the Wisdom schools and the law, has appeared in a new light through the modern study of the Old Testament. With this has gone a changed attitude to the study of prophecy itself. Instead of directing attention to the psychology of prophecy as a religious phenomenon, interest has switched to a study of the prophetic message itself, and its particular background. By placing the prophets upon a pedestal the earlier historians of Israel's religion removed them from their real flesh and blood existence in the life of their people. By regarding them as the creators of all that was most spiritual and ethical in Israel's religion, attention was diverted from their primary role as the messengers of Yahweh who were concerned with the covenant relationship between Yahweh and Israel.[2] It is in their concern with this unique position of Israel before Yahweh, and in the threat of the dissolution of the covenant with a hope of its subsequent restoration, that the heart of the prophetic message is to

---

[1] Cf. G. von Rad, *Theologie des A.T.* II, pp. 48, 218ff.

[2] This is so even when due regard is given to the fact that some of the earliest canonical prophets, viz. Amos, Isaiah and Micah, do not use the term 'covenant' (Heb. *bĕrīth*) in this sense. See below p. 54.

be found. What they achieved was not the averting of the judgment of Yahweh, nor the transformation of Israel's religion into something entirely new, but the awakening of a deeper awareness of what the covenant meant, so that, with the experience of defeat and exile, there might arise a new community, penitent of its past sins, and eager to receive the fulfilment of the gracious promises of a restored covenant. The prophets were first and foremost interpreters of history, and in particular of the course of historical events which meant defeat, suffering and exile for the kingdoms of Israel and Judah, during the eighth, seventh and sixth centuries BC. The great political events which filled their horizons were fraught with significance for them because they were a part of Yahweh's dealings with Israel. By enabling Israel to understand its history in the light of its obligations to the covenant the prophets saved Israel from both arrogance and despair. They assailed any false trust on Israel's part in a divine grace devoid of any moral content, and at the same time they pointed beyond the experience of suffering and defeat to the grace of God, which had first called Israel into being. From the collapse and dissolution of the old covenant order, seen by the prophets to have been brought about as the inevitable result of Israel's disobedience, they pointed forward to a new work of Yahweh in which he would start again and form Israel anew to be his people. The Judaism which arose after the exile therefore was very much interested in the preaching of the pre-exilic prophets, for in it the people found hope for their own existence. The awareness that the judgment had fallen, and that God in his mercy was calling them to a new beginning, was a primary datum of their faith. The tragic history which their ancestors had experienced was not a denial of Yahweh's love for Israel, nor a sign of his impotence to intervene in history. On the contrary this history was seen to be necessary as a part of Yahweh's dealings with Israel, for he was the holy God. It was by taking heed to the message of the prophets that Israel was, after the exile, able to find meaning in its experience and hope for its future. The prophetic interpretation of history was the primary feature which turned the eyes of later generations back to the prophetic writings again and again, and made them a source of understanding and of hope.

II

AMOS AND THE BEGINNINGS OF WRITTEN PROPHECY

THE earliest of the prophets whose words and experiences were recorded and collected, and which have subsequently become canonical, was Amos, whose appearance may be dated about 760 BC. In the extant written record of his preaching it is obvious from the forms and style of utterance that by his time prophecy had attained a position of considerable maturity.[1] Already it had a long history, and in many ways Amos was not dissimilar from the prophets who had preceded him.[2] We are all the more concerned therefore to ask, 'Why does scriptural prophecy begin with him?' We are not entitled to conclude that this is the result of pure chance,[3] but must seek to find something in his message which impressed itself on his hearers, and which vindicated itself in Israel's experience, so that his preaching was made the subject of permanent record. Before we can consider the preaching of Amos, however, we must look at the prophetic activity which had already made a place for itself in Israel's life and religious institutions.

The first clear picture of prophecy in Israel comes to us from the age of Saul, although its manifestations certainly go very

---

[1] Cf. J. Hempel, *Die althebräische Literatur und ihr hellenistisch-jüdisches Nachleben*, Potsdam, 1934, p. 66, 'Amos is no beginning, but already a high point.' A. Bentzen, *Introduction to the Old Testament* (2nd ed.), Copenhagen, 1952, I, p. 193, 'Amos already represents a fully developed style and accordingly presupposes a long tradition, perhaps extending over centuries.'

[2] One of the most radical attempts to make a complete separation between the canonical prophets and the earlier *nĕbhi'im* is that of A. Jepsen, *Nabi. Soziologische Studien zur alttestamentlichen Literatur und Religionsgeschichte*, Munich, 1934. Jepsen denies that the canonical prophets even called themselves *nĕbhi'im*, and argues that the prophetic collections have undergone a 'nabi-istic' redaction.

[3] That it is merely a fortuitous circumstance of Israelite tradition that written prophecy commences with Amos is claimed by H. Graf Reventlow, *Das Amt des Propheten bei Amos* (FRLANT 80), Göttingen, 1962, p. 22. This could only be maintained if no valid reason could be found which explains a new departure with Amos, which is not the case.

27

much farther back in near-eastern history.[1] When it made a firm place for itself in Israelite society it was no unheard-of innovation, but a familiar part of religious life in that ancient world. At many times Israelites must have encountered men with prophetic gifts, such as tradition told of Balaam, and no real purpose is served by arguing whether or not prophecy entered into Israel from Canaan.[2]

In the age of Saul we meet with groups of prophets, wandering in companies and delivering oracles at the request of enquirers who rewarded them suitably. These travelling groups seem not to have been permanently attached to any one place, although they usually rendered their services at a religious assembly in a sanctuary. By the age of David it is clear from the position of Nathan, that individual prophets could rise to great eminence, and play a considerable part in the political affairs of the realm. The oracle of Nathan to David (II Sam. 7), promising to the monarch divine authority and support for his kingship, and the establishing of his sons after him, was of considerable importance for the whole future of Israel. That a genuine historical nucleus lies within this oracle, and that Nathan was an influential figure in David's court cannot be in doubt. This belief in a covenant between Yahweh and the house of David, based on Nathan's oracle, provided a divine authorization for the monarchical State which David introduced, and it formed a continuing basis of the religious and political life of Judah, long after the Davidic empire was broken up at Solomon's death. Thus not only was Nathan a person of considerable significance in the early days of the Israelite State, but one of his oracles became fundamental to the religious tradition of Judah, and played an important part in the rise of the messianic hope.

Further evidence of the influence of prophets on political affairs is found in the case of Ahijah of Shiloh, whose foretelling to Jeroboam of his future position as ruler of the northern part of the Israelite State (I Kings 11.29–39), must be regarded as a strong

---

[1] The question of the prophetic character of Moses cannot be dealt with here, since we have too little historical information to make positive statements about his character and work. That prophetic features appear in his activity can hardly be denied, as the O.T. traditions affirm about him (Deut. 18.18; Hos. 12.14 (EVV 13); cf. Num. 12.6–8).

[2] So G. Hölscher, *Die Propheten*, pp. 140ff. A criticism of such a view is made by J. Lindblom, 'Zur Frage des kanaanäischen Ursprungs des altisraelitischen Prophetismus', *Von Ugarit nach Qumran* (BZAW 77), Berlin, 1958, pp. 89ff., and *Prophecy in Ancient Israel*, pp. 97ff.

incitement to planned rebellion. The numerous stories of prophets associated with Jeroboam illustrate the popular regard for their oracles, and a certain awe at their position in society. The narratives which have grown up around Elijah and Elisha make it difficult to arrive at an exact appraisal of their place in Israel's history. Elijah appeared and checked the worship of Baal in Israel by his defiant challenge to the Baal priests, and by his opposition to the attempt of Jezebel to foster the worship in Israel of Baal-Melqart of Tyre.[1] Elisha's role seems to have been quite intensely nationalistic, and his activity to have been concerned with the constant border struggle between Israel and the Aramaeans in the ninth century BC. Micaiah-ben-Imla stands out in the court of Ahab for his unexpected prediction of disaster for the king (I Kings 22.5–28), over against the overwhelming majority of prophets who foretold a victory for Israel and the safe-keeping of the king in the forthcoming battle.

Besides these outstanding figures, and the information which we have about them, it is quite clear that prophecy was a very prominent and well-accepted part of Israelite religion. Elijah and Elisha were heads of large groups of prophets, who formed a formidable body of supporters for the Yahwistic religion. Baal too was served by a considerable number of such prophets, who naturally found themselves in rivalry to their Yahwistic counterparts.

One of the most valuable advances obtained by modern research into the earlier prophetic activity is the recognition of the great importance of prophets as cult-functionaries.[2] The picture that we have of the developed state of the Israelite priesthood shows a great hierarchy of cult-officials, with different functions each with its own particular status. In earlier times such a well-defined system did not pertain, and a great variety of cult-officials operated at the various sanctuaries. In particular it is clear that no institutional barrier separated the prophet from the priest, and

---

[1] In I Kings 19.10, 14 Elijah accuses Israel of forsaking the covenant, but the introduction of the word 'covenant' is probably an editorial expansion of an original reference to forsaking Yahweh, as some versions attest. See J. A. Montgomery, *I & II Kings* (ICC), Edinburgh, 1951, p. 317. However, the idea of the covenant certainly underlies the language. So J. Gray, *I & II Kings*, London, 1964, pp. 364f.

[2] See above p. 21.

that both together were necessary servants of the great shrines. Such cultic prophets obtained oracular decisions from the deity, and mediated to the worshippers information about the deity's acceptance of, or displeasure at, their offerings and prayers. The composition and delivery of more lengthy oracles was also accomplished, particularly at the great festivals, when issues of local or national importance would be dealt with. Such prophets were feared and respected, if not always admired, and the narratives of the Books of Samuel and Kings show the great interest and importance that was attached to their words.

These prophets were the spokesmen of Yahweh to his people, and, from the examples which we have, it seems that the majority of their oracles were directed towards individuals. Often this would be at the individual person's request, who sought a particular favour or answer from Yahweh, and who made use of the prophet's services to this end. For this service it was normal for the worshipper to reward the prophet with a fee of some kind. We have many examples, however, of prophetic oracles being given unsought, when the prophet believed himself commissioned to deliver a message of special personal or national importance. The prophet was a specialist in prayer, and a notable aspect of his work was to intercede on behalf of worshippers, or even on behalf of a much larger group.[1]

All of this activity was comprehended within the normal pattern of cultic life in Israel, and its main difference from what had previously existed in Canaanite society, was that Israel's prophets were the servants of Yahweh, and their task was defined by the needs of the covenant as the basis of Israel's life. Such was at least ideally the case, although we cannot suppose that any rigorous orthodoxy could be enforced. The overall object for which prophets existed was to maintain the proper welfare (Heb. *shālōm*) of Israel as Yahweh's people. This certainly did not mean, however, that they only prophesied 'salvation', and had no words of judg-

---

[1] A. R. Johnson, *The Cultic Prophet in Ancient Israel*, pp. 58ff. H. W. Hertzberg, 'Sind die Propheten Fürbitter ?', *Tradition und Situation. Studien zur alttestamentlichen Prophetie,* ed. E. Würthwein and O. Kaiser, Göttingen, 1963, pp. 63ff., argues that in the classical prophets no official function as intercessors can be spoken of. The privilege of intercession belonged to any prominent man of God in Ancient Israel. Whilst this was so, it seems particularly to have been the responsibility of prophets.

ment to deliver to Israel and to Israelites. We have several instances recorded of dire warnings of Yahweh's judgment given through the mouths of prophets.[1] By rooting out sinners from the people, and by condemning offences against Yahweh's holy will, the prophets worked for the overall maintenance of a right relationship between Yahweh and his people. So also prophetic oracles against foreign nations could be a means of enhancing the blessing towards Israel, by prophesying Israel's exaltation and the defeat and downfall of nations which threatened her.

The power of such oracles was exemplary of the great power that was believed to exist in the spoken word. Oracles were not mere words, but forceful weapons which could secure the attainment of the blessing or curse which they contained.[2] Thus the prophet was believed to have the power of securing victory or defeat for Israel. Words were powerful instruments in attaining certain ends, and this was particularly so when delivered by a prophet who invoked the name of his God. This must not be taken to imply that the prophets were able to attain the fulfilment of all their wishes, but it must be borne in mind that, as Yahweh's servants, they were intermediaries between the divine and human worlds. They claimed a communion with the divine which was believed to give them special powers of insight and a particular potency in prayer.

Such prophets were nationalists since they belonged to Israel, and sought to serve the true interests of its cult, but they were not impeded from delivering oracles against nations beyond the borders of Israel. Although it was usual for them to receive some payments for their service, this was true of all cult-ministrants, and can in no way be used to level an accusation of professionalism against such prophets. Although much of their behaviour seems strange and even irrational, we cannot dismiss their contribution to the religious life and development of Israel as of small account. Much of the prophetic element in the Psalter must owe its origin to these cult-prophets,[3] and they gave expression to many of the highest ideals cherished by Israel. Their part in shaping the

---

[1] E.g., I Kings 13.2–3, 21–22; 14.10–11; 16.2–4; 21.21–24; 22.17.
[2] Cf. J. Pedersen, *Israel* I–II, Copenhagen, 1926, pp. 165ff.
[3] S. Mowinckel, *Psalmenstudien* II, pp. 30ff.; *The Psalms in Israel's Worship* II, pp. 58ff.

development of Israel's cult-liturgy, and in inculcating a right understanding of the nature and demands of Yahweh was very important. In an age of considerable confusion and diversity in religion, we may believe that some of these anonymous prophets were faithful and sincere upholders of the covenant tradition of Israel. In the Autumn Festival, as it developed in the Jerusalem temple, it is very probable that cultic prophets had a part to play, and this must also have been the case at other of the major sanctuaries, as well as at other festival occasions. What kind of role may have been played by such prophets in the covenant ceremonies of Israel in the pre-monarchic period is very much more obscure and uncertain, but even here we cannot dismiss the possibility that they had a contribution to make. In any case during the period of the monarchy it is certain that prophets were accorded an official position in the Israelite cult. Long before any prophetic writings were given canonical status it appears that individual prophets could be regarded as official spokesmen of the covenant.

A certain ambiguity exists in the term 'cultic prophet', because of the very wide range of meaning which is covered by the term 'cult'. It may mean simply that Israel's early prophets operated within the context of the established forms of worship of the people. In this sense we may claim that all the prophets were cultic prophets, since their activity was in some measure always a public one. Only a prophet who reacted against the established worship of his day, and who rejected it, could then deserve the title of a non-cultic prophet. We have no evidence that any of the early prophets, or prophetic groups, did this. Even the prophets whose writings have been made canonical cannot be called non-cultic since, although many of them criticized the cult which they found, they still made use of its festivals and public occasions. They did not reject altogether the possibility of any cult. The term 'cultic prophet', however, has usually been taken in a narrower sense to denote prophets who held official positions on the staff of certain sanctuaries. There cannot be any doubt that some prophets did hold such established positions, and were a part of the permanent organization of resident cult-functionaries at Israel's shrines. Along with the other members of the cult-staff they received their livelihood from the gifts of the worshippers whom they served. Whilst such prophets undoubtedly existed, it is certain that not all the early prophets of Israel were of such a kind. The picture that presents itself to us is rather of a considerable variety of prophetic activity. At one time different kinds of prophets seem to have been recognized, with distinctions between the seer (Heb. *ḥōzēh, rō'ēh*) and the prophet (Heb. *nābhi'*), which were later ignored (I Sam. 9.9). Many of the prophets remained free of any permanent association with a royal court, or a sanctuary.[1] Such 'free', or 'charismatic' prophets were none the less regarded as Yahweh's spokesmen. The large guilds of prophets seem to have been self-contained communities, sharing a common board and owning a common allegiance to their 'father'. This does not mean that such prophets were aloof from the cult, or opposed to its practices, but simply that they conducted themselves with a measure of freedom towards the established sanctuaries. Prophecy, therefore, in early Israel seems to have been delivered by a variety of specialists in the techniques of divination, prayer and religious instruction. Some prophets held official positions at the sanctuaries or court, whilst many of them pursued a less organized existence.

It is most probable that all the prophets regarded their work as a divine vocation, and that they claimed to have received some kind of call to the task of prophesying.[2] This is reasonably certain irrespective of the etymology which we adopt for the term *nābhi'*.[3] Just how this call came to them must have varied immensely in individual cases, and in some instances may have been no more than a consequence of social pressure or family tradition. In other cases it is likely that some dramatic religious experience resulted in the adoption of a prophet's vocation, as we find described by some of the canonical prophets.[4]

[1] Cf. J. Lindblom, *Prophecy in Ancient Israel*, pp. 206f.; A. R. Johnson, *The Cultic Prophet in Ancient Israel*, pp. 22 note, 74 note.

[2] Cf. E. Würthwein, 'Amos Studien', *ZAW* 62, 1949–50, pp. 25f.

[3] The etymology of the Hebrew noun *nābhi'* is not completely assured, but its root must have some relation to the Akkadian *nabu* 'to call, announce'. The form of the noun may be construed either in an active sense, thus giving the meaning 'caller, announcer', or in a passive sense meaning 'one who is called'. The latter interpretation is preferred by W. F. Albright, *From the Stone Age to Christianity* (2nd ed.), New York, 1957, p. 303. Probability, however, seems to favour the former interpretation. See on the question, A. R. Johnson, *The Cultic Prophet in Ancient Israel*, p. 24 note.

[4] We must also recognize the fact that a person who was already a prophet could subsequently receive a call by Yahweh to fulfil a special task committed

It may be useful at this point to summarize some of the important points which result from the study of early Israelite prophecy and its cultic background. It cannot be maintained that such prophetic activity was necessarily on a low spiritual level, or that such prophets were mere professionals with no genuine conviction. Neither can we claim that such prophets did not experience any genuine call to their work. Further, it cannot be accepted any longer that the pre-canonical prophets proclaimed only a message of salvation for Israel, with no threat of judgment, and that prophecies of judgment were reserved only for foreign nations who endangered Israel's welfare.[1] The very desire on the part of scholars to stress the spiritual greatness of the canonical prophets has often resulted in an unconscious tendency to denigrate the work and activity of their predecessors. This is not justified, and in fact the oracles of the earliest two canonical prophets, Amos and Hosea, should warn us against such an approach. Both of these prophets refer to the appearance of prophets in Israel as tokens of Yahweh's concern for his people, and they show that such prophetic preaching took the form of warnings of the divine punishment and judgment.[2] The fact that Hosea could also criticize certain prophets for their unfaithfulness to their task[3] must not be allowed to mislead us into neglecting the positive evaluation of the *nĕbhi'im* that the earliest canonical prophets made. This fact alone shows the danger of a simple identification of the false prophets, who are especially blamed by Micah and Jeremiah, with the successors of the early prophetic guilds of the time of Saul.[4]

---

to him. Cf. G. A. Danell, 'Var Amos verkligen en nabi?' *SEA* 16, 1951, pp. 16f. We may sometimes therefore need to allow for a difference between being called to the office of *nābhi'*, and being given a special commission by Yahweh.

[1] So recently R. Hentschke, *Die Stellung der vorexilischen Schriftpropheten zum Kultus* (BZAW 75), 1957, Berlin, p. 152. That the earlier *nĕbhi'im* proclaimed a message of judgment as well as salvation is argued by A. H. J. Gunneweg, 'Erwägungen zu Amos 7.14', *ZTK* 57, 1960, p. 7. There is adequate evidence in the Old Testament to prove such to have been the case. Cf. also H. Graf Reventlow, *Das Amt des Propheten bei Amos*, pp. 19f.

[2] Amos 2.11–12; 3.7–8; Hos. 9.7–8; 12.11, 14 (EVV 10, 13).

[3] Hos. 4.5.

[4] So L. W. Batten, *The Hebrew Prophet*, London, 1905, p. 58. The problem of false prophecy is a very complex one, and is not susceptible to simple explanations. G. von Rad, 'Die falschen Propheten', *ZAW* 51, 1933, pp. 109ff., identifies the false prophets as cult-prophets, who were preachers of

No simple contrast between the errors of the *nĕbhī'īm* and the truth of the canonical prophets can be presumed, and the distinctiveness of the canonical prophets lies elsewhere than in the claim that they reversed the message of their forerunners.

We must bear in mind this general background of prophecy in Israel when we endeavour to understand the significance of Amos. Since he is the first of the prophets whose activity and preaching were recorded and compiled into a book, it is a matter of considerable theological importance to ask what was distinctive about him and his particular prophecies. What led to the preservation of his oracles, whilst those of earlier prophets never attained such a canonical status?

It is fortunate for us that Amos is not only the earliest of the writing prophets, but that the book that bears his name is itself a classic among the prophets. It is brief, well-preserved and it raises many of the most important issues in a striking way. In particular Amos provides us with information about his call, and about the conflict which arose over his preaching in his own day. Amos appeared at the sanctuary of Bethel and delivered there an oracle foretelling the doom of the sanctuary, the royal household and in fact the end of the entire kingdom of Israel. These shattering words inevitably aroused great consternation, and summoned Amaziah, the chief priest of the royal sanctuary of Bethel, to take action. He promptly forbad Amos to deliver any further oracles in the sanctuary, for the good order of which he was responsible:

> And Amaziah said to Amos, 'O seer, go, flee away to the land of Judah, and eat bread there, and prophesy there; but never again prophesy at Bethel, for it is the king's sanctuary, and it is a royal temple.'
>
> (Amos 7.12–13.)

These words of Amaziah sound very animated and even

---

salvation, and especially intercessors for Israel. This is too dogmatic a scheme, however, and no rigid identification of the cult-prophets as 'false' in the eyes of the canonical prophets is justified. The phenomenon of false prophecy must have been inherent in the prophetic movement from earliest times, and no fixed canon of 'truth' could be permanently established. Cf. G. Quell, *Wahre und falsche Propheten*, Gütersloh, 1952, esp. pp. 206ff.; E. Osswald, *Falsche Prophetie im A.T.*, Tübingen, 1962.

scornful of the position of Amos. E. Würthwein[1] has, however, sought to remove the sting out of them by interpreting them as advice, rather than as a contemptuous attack. The phrase 'eat bread' means no more than 'live, sustain yourself', and does not necessarily contain any overtones of disrespect, accusing Amos of professionalism.[2] After all Amaziah himself earned his keep from his priestly office. The injunction to flee to Judah may have been intended to carry the significance that Amos's words would be permitted there (he was a Judean), whilst the King of Israel, to whom Amaziah was responsible, could not possibly tolerate such prophecies in his kingdom. Würthwein then goes even further in suggesting that Amaziah may have had a genuine regard for Amos, and, whilst being compelled to maintain order in his sanctuary, was concerned to prevent any violence being done to a prophet whom he held in respect. For a parallel case of such an attitude Würthwein compares the experience of Jeremiah in the Jerusalem temple (Jer. 36).

In spite of this attempt to mitigate the violence of Amaziah's words, it seems to be very improbable, in the light of Amos's reply, that Amaziah displayed any real regard for Amos, or his message. Whilst it is not impossible that the prophet should have taken genuine advice as an affront to his divine commission, it is much more likely that Amos regarded the arrogant scorn of the priest as a rejection of Yahweh's word and messenger. Amos replied to this prohibition by referring to the circumstances of his call, which made it impossible for him to obey Amaziah's command, and which, incidentally, shows that Amos was a person who had no need to live by his prophesying:

> Then Amos answered Amaziah, 'I was no prophet, nor a member of a prophetic guild; but I was a herdsman, and a dresser of sycamore trees, and Yahweh took me from following the flock, and Yahweh said to me. Go, prophesy to my people Israel.'
>
> (Amos 7.14–15.)

This is followed by a particularly fearful threat of judgment on Amaziah and his family, because he has dared to oppose the mes-

[1] E. Würthwein, 'Amos Studien', *ZAW* 62, 1949–50, pp. 19ff.
[2] Cf. L. Köhler, *Lexicon in Veteris Testamenti Libros*, Leiden, 1953, p. 43.

sage which Yahweh has commissioned the prophet to deliver. The reply of Amos to Amaziah is of great importance for a consideration of his understanding of his relationship to the earlier *nĕbhī'īm*. It was frequently claimed by interpreters that Amos was here refusing to identify himself as a *nābhī'*, or as a member of one of the *nābhī'*-guilds. Such an interpretation is implicit in the translation adopted by the RSV. It has, however, been convincingly opposed by H. H. Rowley,[1] who argues that the Hebrew text of verse 14a, which is made up of two nominal clauses, can be translated by a past tense, and be understood to refer to past events. Thus Amos did not deny that he was a prophet when he spoke to Amaziah, but was referring back to the circumstances which led to his becoming one. From having no prophetic task, or association, he was summoned by Yahweh to deliver his message, and so he had no right to disobey his divinely given orders. Such a translation of the Hebrew text is permissible, but apart from the grammatical possibilities, it is the interpretation which does fullest justice to other statements which Amos made concerning prophecy. 1. In his reply to Amaziah Amos uses the verb 'prophesy' (Heb. *hinnābhē'*), which shows that he understood

---

[1] H. H. Rowley, 'Was Amos a Nabi?', O. *Eissfeldt Festschrift zum 60 Geburtstage,* Halle, 1947, pp. 191ff. Rowley's interpretation is followed by A. H. J. Gunneweg, 'Erwägungen zu Amos 7, 14', *ZTK* 57, 1960, pp. 2f.; R. Hentschke, *Die Stellung der vorexilischen Schriftpropheten zum Kultus,* pp. 150f.; H. Graf Reventlow, *Das Amt des Propheten bei Amos,* pp. 14ff.; I. Engnell, 'Profetismens ursprung och uppkomst. Ett gammaltestamentligt grundproblem', *Religion och Bibel* VIII, Lund, 1949, p. 16; J. P. Hyatt, 'Amos', *Peake's Commentary on the Bible* (rev. ed.), London, 1962, p. 624. It is opposed by S. Lehming, 'Erwägungen zu Amos' *ZTK* 55, 1958, pp. 145ff., who endeavours to show that Amos separated himself from the earlier *nĕbhī'īm*, since his message was of woe, whilst theirs was one of salvation. Cf. also G. A. Danell, 'Var Amos verkligen en nabi?', *SEA* 16, 1951, pp. 13ff., who argues that Amos dissociated himself from the professional prophets because of his very special commission. Danell says, 'He is a *nābhī'* extra ordinem' (p. 15). We may compare also J. Lindblom, *Prophecy in Ancient Israel,* p. 184, 'Amos was a prophet, but not a prophet in the sense in which Amaziah used the word, referring to the fact that Amos had for the time being attached himself to the sanctuary prophets at Bethel; he was not a "ben-nabi", i.e. he was not a member of an ordinary association of temple prophets.' G. R. Driver, 'Amos vii:14', *ExpT* 67, 1955–6, pp. 91f., has sought to understand the Hebrew *lō'* in verse 14 as an asseverative, meaning, 'Am I not a prophet, for Yahweh called me . . . . ?' Cf. also G. R. Driver, 'Waw explicative in Amos vii:14', *ExpT* 68, 1956–7, p. 302, and P. R. Ackroyd, 'Amos vii:14', *ExpT* 68, 1956–7, p. 94.

that what he was doing could only be described as 'prophesying'.[1]
2. Amos could not have rejected all the earlier prophets such as
Nathan, Elijah and Micaiah-ben-Imla. 3. In Amos 3.7–8 Amos
values the prophets in a very positive fashion, and this oracle
describes very suitably the divine compulsion to prophesy by
which Amos justified his message to Amaziah.

We can only draw one conclusion from this, and that is that
Amos regarded himself as a *nābhî'*, and that in his words to Amaziah he was referring to the remarkable circumstances of his call
to this task. Before this call he had had no prophetic associations,
but had earned his living as a shepherd (Heb. *bōqēr*; cf. 1.1 where
the term *nōqēdh* is used), and by looking after a type of wild fig
(sycamore) tree. The attempt on the part of Engnell to find in the
term *nōqēdh* a reference to a class of cultic personnel[2] must be
termed a failure.[3] It simply denotes a shepherd, who may, or may
not, have been in the employ of a sanctuary, and in Amos's case
we must conclude that he was not. Such an occupation may not
have been a particularly poor one, so that Amos may have been a
person of some means, and an incidental point in his reply to
Amaziah would have been that he had no necessity to earn his keep
by his prophesying.

This insistence by Amos upon the fact of his divine call is held
out by him to Amaziah as the sole authority and justification for
his message. Yet, in this conviction that his prophetic standing was
the result of a special call-experience directly received from Yahweh, Amos was not claiming a new authority for his words which
other prophets could not have paralleled. We have argued already
that it was customary in Israel for prophets to take up their work
at the receipt of a special call to do so. Wherein then did Amos
differ from them? We can only conclude that it was in the intensity
of his conviction, and in his willingness to submit his entire
personality to the authority of his divine call. Amaziah, as priest-

[1] The attempt of S. Lehming, *op. cit.*, pp. 146ff., to argue that the verb
hinnābhē' was used in a wider and less technical sense than the noun *nābhî'*
cannot be accepted. There is no evidence to justify such a separation of the
two forms derived from the same stem. Cf. A. H. J. Gunneweg, 'Erwägungen
zu Amos 7.14', *ZTK* 57, 1960, pp. 4f.

[2] I. Engnell, *Studies in Divine Kingship in the Ancient Near East*, Uppsala,
1947, pp. 87f., and 'Profetismens ursprung och uppkomst', *Religion och Bibel*
VIII, p. 15. Cf. also A. S. Kapelrud, *Central Ideas in Amos*, Oslo, 1956, p. 6.

[3] G. A. Danell, *art. cit.*, p. 8.

in-charge of the royal shrine, was usually able to have his orders carried out, even over the prophets who appeared there. Yet with Amos he encountered a new integrity and firmness of purpose, which he could not manipulate to his will. Here was one who was not different from other prophets in claiming another, and more weighty, authority than theirs, but who differed solely in the fact that he believed this divine authorization to be enough.

The clear recognition on the part of Amos that he was a *nābhī'*, and that he had had many predecessors, shows that the prophet himself was not conscious of introducing a new kind of prophecy. The scandal of his activity to Amaziah existed in the message which he delivered, and it is here that his great originality lay. But how did his message differ from that of his predecessors? We have already pointed out that it is false to suppose that the earlier prophets had only prophesied salvation for Israel and Israelites. It is wrong therefore to suppose that the novelty in the preaching of Amos lay in his prophecies of judgment, which contrasted with the optimistic prophecies of salvation of those who had preceded him.[1] By prophesying the coming divine judgment on Israel, Amos was in line with some of the warnings which had been given by prophets before, as he himself recognized.[2] Thus the mere fact of preaching judgment was not new with Amos.[3] What does seem

[1] This is argued by R. Hentschke, *op. cit.*, p. 152. E. Würthwein, 'Amos Studien', *ZAW* 62, pp. 27ff., adheres to the view that the *nĕbhī'īm* were preachers of salvation, and claims that Amos first operated as such a *nābhī'*-preacher of salvation. Subsequently he became convinced of the inappropriateness of such a message, when he sensed the divine warning of coming judgment. Thereupon he turned to proclaim this coming doom. This change-over from a message of doom to one of salvation Würthwein traces in the series of visions received by Amos (Amos 7.1–3, 4–6, 7–9; 8.1–3; 9.1–4). In the first two of these Amos saw disasters which were about to fall on Israel, and interceded for the nation. The disasters were thereby averted. After this point Würthwein believes that Amos became convinced of the futility of further intercession on Israel's behalf and became a preacher of doom. That Amos ever appeared as a preacher of salvation in this way loses any support once we reject the view that the *nĕbhī'īm* only preached salvation. It is very probable, however, that the visions bear some relation to Amos's call. So A. Weiser, *Die Prophetie des Amos* (BZAW 53), Giessen, 1929, pp. 21ff., 51ff., 73ff. Cf. also his commentary, *Das Buch der zwölf Kleinen Propheten* I, ATD 24 (2 Aufl.), Göttingen, 1956, p. 182, and G. von Rad, *Theologie des A.T.* II, p. 141.

[2] Amos 2.11f.

[3] This is convincingly argued by A. H. J. Gunneweg, 'Erwägungen zu Amos 7.14', *ZTK* 57, pp. 7ff.

to have been new, however, was the preaching of a judgment which meant the end of Israel as the people of Yahweh:

Hear this word which I take up over you in lamentation, O house of Israel:

'Fallen, no more to rise,
   is the virgin Israel;
forsaken on her land,
   with none to raise her up.'
                    (Amos 5, 1–2.)

Thus Yahweh God showed me: behold a basket of summer fruit. And he said, 'Amos, what do you see?' And I said, 'A basket of summer fruit.' Then Yahweh said to me,

'The end has come upon my people Israel;
I will never again pass by them.'
                    (Amos 8.1–2; cf. also 3.2; 9.7–8.)

Earlier prophets had proclaimed the divine judgment on sinners within Israel, but the message which Amos brought meant a judgment which embraced the entire Northern Kingdom, and which implied an end of the covenant between Yahweh and Israel. The new feature in the preaching of Amos, therefore, was not simply that he prophesied doom, since others before him had also delivered oracles of judgment, but that the doom which Amos preached meant the end of Israel.[1] This, so far as we know, was something which none of his predecessors had done. Earlier prophets had delivered oracles foretelling Yahweh's punishment on individual sinners, but had not foreseen Yahweh's judgment falling upon the whole nation, and resulting in the dissolution of the covenant. The originality of the message of Amos lay not in the fact of a preaching of judgment, but in the extent and significance of the judgment which he preached.

It is important in this regard to recognize a connexion between the threats contained in this prophetic proclamation of judgment and the curses threatened in the covenant cult. The Autumn Festival, which reaffirmed the promises and demands of the covenant, contained a public recital of the covenant law, followed by a declaration of blessings upon the obedient and curses for the

---

[1] Cf. C. Westermann, *Grundformen prophetischer Rede*, p. 99, who argues that Amos has developed the earlier form of a judgment proclamation upon an individual into a judgment proclamation on the entire nation.

disobedient.[1] It is possible that such blessings and curses were even made the subject of prophetic oracles delivered during the festival period.[2] In this case the covenant cult itself invested the prophetic office with a special function in its celebrations. The curse of the law was a real factor in the Israelite cult, and such a curse threatened disease, famine, exile and disaster for all who violated the demands of the covenant. The covenant tradition of Israel, therefore, as it was maintained in the cult, held out the possibility of divine judgment for individual members of the covenant people, and even for the people as a whole. This was at least ideally the case, although we must make allowances for two factors. The first is that during the period of the monarchy the covenant tradition was only maintained by the cult in a very broken and modified form. Secondly it is quite intelligible that the sterner aspects of the covenant demands were prone to suffer neglect, and a failure on Israel's part to take them seriously. In such a context, where the cult tended to obscure the threat of Yahweh's wrath against disobedience to his covenant, Amos arose to present his message. In his words a new urgency lent strength to his insistence that if Israel neglected the covenant, Yahweh would not, but would punish the iniquities of his people with the curse:

> You only have I known
>   of all the families of the earth;
> therefore I will punish you
>   for all your iniquities.
> (Amos 3.2.)

The very presupposition of the prophecy of doom which Amos brought is the existence of the covenant relationship between Yahweh and Israel, and the crowning woe is to be the ending of that relationship. Israel has forfeited all its privileges. Thus Amos,

---

[1] Cf. Deut. 27; 28; Lev. 26. On the Blessings and Curses see H. Graf Reventlow, *Das Heiligkeitsgesetz* (WMANT 6), Munich, 1961, pp. 142ff., and *Das Amt des Propheten bei Amos*, pp. 75ff.; M. Noth, 'Die mit des Gesetzes Werken umgehen, die sind unter dem Fluch', *Ges. Stud.z.A.T.*, pp. 155ff. Noth argues that the cult originally proclaimed only curses and that the promises of blessing have been subsequently introduced. For the tradition of a threat contained in the covenant cult see also A. Weiser, *The Psalms*, pp. 32f., and R. Vuilleumier, *La tradition cultuelle d'Israël dans la prophétie d'Amos et d'Osée* (CT 45), Neuchâtel, 1960, pp. 81f.

[2] H. Graf Reventlow, *Das Amt des Propheten bei Amos*, pp. 75ff.

in his message of doom, was able to use the covenant tradition as the very ground of his proclamation.[1] Just how far the curse of the law was ever visualized as actually threatening the break-up of the covenant relationship we do not know, but it was certainly held out as a possibility.[2] Amos has taken this threat, and has given it a radical significance. He was not thinking any longer of a purge of sinners within the covenant, such as earlier prophets had foretold, but declared that the entire covenant people had become sinful. He could not stand within the covenant to prop it up, but had to move outside it, since Yahweh himself was Lord of the covenant, and was about to bring it to an end.

There is with Amos, therefore, both a measure of continuity with the prophets of the past, as he himself recognized, and also an important new feature. Amos foretold the end of Israel as Yahweh's covenant people, and this judgment was eventually seen to have fallen upon the Northern Kingdom in 721 BC, with the collapse of Israel under the Assyrian assault. In Judah the old Israelite tradition was maintained in an independent kingdom until 587 BC, when Jerusalem was conquered by Nebuchadnezzar. The preaching of Amos provided a warning to both Israel and Judah which prepared them to receive these disasters by insisting that the covenant contained a threat upon any disobedience. Its privileges were matched by corresponding demands, which Israel had not fulfilled, and as a consequence the covenant itself demanded

[1] H. Graf Reventlow, *Das Amt des Propheten bei Amos, passim*, goes further than this, and claims that Amos was consciously using forms of oracular delivery, which had their origin in the covenant cult. He claims that Amos was intentionally fulfilling the role of the prophetic office which had grown up in the particular context of that cult. He argues that the Blessing Ritual (Amos 9.13–15), the Oracle against the Nations (Amos 1.3–2.6) and the Curse Ritual (Amos 4.6–11) all stem from the 'official' character of Amos's prophecy in which he fulfilled the role of the prophet of the covenant.

This goes beyond the justifiable evidence. Even if the actual forms of Amos's preaching do go back to such cultic prototypes, this is insufficient ground for claiming that Amos was intending to fulfil such a role. Identity of form does not mean identity of office, since stereotyped forms and language have a remarkable tenacity in religious circles of all kinds. It is doubtful, however, whether such forms were as fully preserved as Graf Reventlow maintains since there are significant variations from any definite cultic prototype. Further we must consider the radical nature of the message of doom which Amos brought. He has moved outside the covenant to some extent by his warning of its impending dissolution.

[2] Cf. Ex. 19.5–6 (E) for the contingent nature of the Sinaitic covenant.

that Israel should be punished. Amos did not bring a new morality, nor a new doctrine of God, but he reawakened in a radical way a sense of the reality of Yahweh and of his expectations of his people.

This continuity with the past, with a sudden and original new departure on the part of the prophet, is well exemplified in Amos's Oracle against the Nations (Amos 1.3–2.6).[1] This 'Execration Oracle'[2] is very probably modelled upon a cultic prototype, and was composed as a single unit.[3] The climax of the whole series of condemnations is found in the saying against Israel, which is the most original part of the entire presentation. After having roundly condemned the neighbouring nations for their sins, a proceeding which would have been familiar enough to the prophet's hearers, he turns upon Israel, and avers that this people also must suffer divine wrath. This does not mean that Amos did not seriously intend the woes upon the other nations, but it does mean that he consciously intended the climax of the whole oracle to be found in its concern with his own nation.[4] Amos was able to take an old form and fill it with a new content.

The new feature that came into prophecy with Amos was the foretelling of the end of Yahweh's covenant relationship to Israel, and it was especially on this account that his oracles were preserved and ultimately given canonical status. He foretold the judgments of defeat and exile through which Israel had to pass in consequence of its disobedience to the covenant. With this radical message of doom went a renewed insistence upon the righteousness

[1] Whether Amos 1.2 belongs to the oracle is a matter of debate. It certainly belongs to a particular cultic tradition, and occurs elsewhere in Joel 4.16 (EVV 3.16) and Jer. 25.30. It is always to be regarded as a possibility, therefore, that it has been inserted subsequently by an editor into Amos's work. On the other hand it fits very well as the opening line of an oracle which was delivered by a Judean prophet, so that no absolute ground for denying it to Amos exists. So A. Bentzen, 'The Ritual Background of Amos 1.2–2.16', *OTS* 8, Leiden, 1950, p. 96.

[2] A. Bentzen *op. cit.*, pp. 89ff. Cf. also F. Hesse, 'Wurzelt die prophetische Gerichtsrede im israelitischen Kult?', *ZAW* 65, 1953, pp. 48ff.

[3] The Judah oracle shows obvious traces of 'deuteronomistic' editing, and may be a subsequent insertion. It is possible that the present form of the oracle represents a replacement by the hand of an editor of an original saying which was lost. So A. S. Kapelrud, *Central Ideas in Amos*, pp. 29f.

[4] A. Weiser, *Die Prophetie des Amos*, pp. 85ff., and *Kleinen Propheten* I, pp. 135ff., argues that the whole point of this oracle is to be found in the Israel saying, and that the woes on the other nations are used as an introduction.

of Yahweh, and a realization that no worship could please him, which was not expressive of obedience to his covenant law. The fact that canonical prophecy begins with Amos, therefore, finds its explanation in the particular attitude that Amos adopted towards the covenant, as the basis of Yahweh's dealings with Israel and his threats concerning it. The fact that beyond the judgment Amos foretold a new beginning of Yahweh's covenant-mercies (Amos 9.11–12) does not primarily concern us in this context, but must be left until we come to consider the question of the prophetic eschatology.

III

THE ELECTION OF ISRAEL IN THE PRE-EXILIC PROPHETS

WE have argued in the preceding chapter that the originality of Amos was not in his introduction of a new ethical standard, nor in the proclamation of a new doctrine of God, but in his declaration of what Yahweh was about to do with Israel. The message of doom, with which written prophecy commences, was delivered in the context of the particular relationship which was understood to exist between Yahweh and Israel. Although Amos declared that Yahweh would punish the sins of other nations, the focus of his attention was upon what Yahweh was about to do with Israel. This is not simply because Amos was a Judean himself, and so belonged to the covenant people, but because he believed that Israel stood in a unique relationship to Yahweh. We must ask then how Amos conceived this unique relationship between Yahweh and Israel to have come about. An answer to this question is provided by the prophet himself:

> Yet I destroyed the Amorite before them,
>   whose height was like the height of the cedars,
>   and who was a strong as the oaks;
> I destroyed his fruit above,
>   and his roots beneath.
> Also I brought you up out of the land of Egypt,
>   and led you forty years in the wilderness,
>   to possess the land of the Amorite.
> (Amos 2.9–10; cf. 9.7.)

This saying shows us a part of the religious tradition which Amos inherited, and which was fundamental to his understanding of the condition of Israel. It refers back to the exodus story of the deliverance from slavery in Egypt, and to a time spent in the desert before the conquest of Canaan. In these events Yahweh was regarded as the chief actor, who had shown his favour towards Israel by delivering them in this way. We may thus speak of it as an election tradition, even though Amos himself does not use the word 'to choose, elect' (Heb. *bāḥar*).[1] Israel had become the people of Yahweh, because he had intervened in the affairs of history on their behalf, taking them to himself as a people and giving them their land. In response to this divine favour shown to them, the people were summoned to live in accordance with their elect state. The persistent failure to do this was the reason why Israel, in the declarations of Amos, had incurred the fearful judgment of Yahweh, which was about to fall.

The tradition that Israel had become the people of Yahweh through divine election at the exodus was dominant in Amos's understanding of who Yahweh was, and what he required of his people. Such a tradition was undoubtedly paramount for Israel as a whole, since it occurs again and again in the canonical prophets, and frequently appears as the foundation of a demand for righteousness and loyalty on Israel's part:

> When Israel was a child, I loved him,
>> and out of Egypt I called my son.
>>> (Hos. 11.1.)

> I am Yahweh your God
>> from the land of Egypt;
> I will again make you dwell in tents,
>> as in the days of the appointed feast.
>>> (Hos. 12.10 [EVV 9].)

> I am Yahweh your God
>> from the land of Egypt;
> you know no God but me,
>> and besides me there is no saviour.
>>> (Hos. 13.4; cf. also 7.16; 8.13; 9.3; 11.5.)

[1] The verb *bāḥar* = 'to choose, elect' first appears in use to express Yahweh's action towards Israel in the Deuteronomic literature. Cf. G. von Rad, *Das Gottesvolk im Deuteronomium* (BWANT III:11), Stuttgart, 1929, p. 28; T. C. Vriezen, *Die Erwählung Israels nach dem Alten Testament* (ATANT 24), Zürich, 1953, p. 47; G. E. Mendenhall, 'Election', *IDB* II, p. 79a. Before the appearance of the Deuteronomic literature, however, the term was invested with a particular religious significance through its use in the Jerusalem tradition of Yahweh's election of David, and of Mount Zion to be his dwelling-place. Cf. K. Koch, 'Zur Geschichte der Erwählungsvorstellung in Israel', *ZAW* 67, 1955, pp. 205ff., and also G. E. Mendenhall, p. 78a. Mendenhall suggests that the author of Deuteronomy derived the idea of describing Yahweh's relationship to Israel as an election from a practice already current in some unknown circle (p. 79a). The basic notion of Yahweh's unique relationship to Israel is certainly extremely old, even though it was not until the appearance of Deuteronomy that this particular linguistic label came to be applied to it.

By Hosea Israel was regarded as in a relationship to Yahweh which took its origin in the gracious election of Yahweh, when he called Israel out of Egypt to be his people. Both Amos and Hosea understood their mission in the light of the particular privileges and responsibility of the people to whom they preached. Yahweh was no strange God, and Israel stood in no need of hearing a new teaching about him. On the contrary the people were guilty of behaving disloyally towards the God who had in the past revealed himself to them and who had shown such favour to their ancestors by delivering them out of Egypt. They had repeatedly neglected their own obligations towards the privileged relationship in which they stood. These prophets were not concerned to introduce a new demand of Yahweh, but were intent upon reminding the people of what was, or at least should have been, well-known to them.

Sometimes, especially in Hosea, the tradition of Israel's election is presented as an election in the desert:

> It was I who knew you in the wilderness,
>   in the land of drought.
>   (Hos. 13.5; cf. 2.16 [EVV 14]; 9.10; Jer. 2.2f.; 31.2f.)

This has been claimed to represent a tradition about Israel's origins, which was at one time quite separate from that of the exodus.[1] That this was so, however, seems to be very improbable, since the exodus tradition itself included a reference to a period spent in the wilderness (Amos 2.10). It seems in every way more likely that the theme of Israel's origin in the wilderness belonged inseparably to the theme of the exodus, and arose because of the immense importance of a period spent at Kadesh in the desert, by those Hebrews who escaped out of Egypt.[2] Here there was first brought together a covenant community of tribes, pledged in loyalty to Yahweh, but which were almost certainly not yet twelve in number, and had not yet adopted the name Israel. Nevertheless it was these Yahweh worshippers who became a vital and formative influence in the development of Israel as the covenant people

---

[1] R. Bach, *Die Erwählung Israels in der Wüste*, Dissertation, Bonn, 1952. Cf. *TLZ* 78, 1953, col. 687. For the tradition of a sojourn in the desert see also M. Noth, *Überlieferungsgeschichte des Pentateuch*, rep. Stuttgart, 1960, pp. 48ff.; *Exodus*, London, 1961, pp. 12ff.; *A History of Israel*, pp. 110ff.

[2] W. Beyerlin, *Herkunft und Geschichte der ältesten Sinaitraditionen*, Tübingen, 1961, pp. 165ff.; M. L. Newman, *The People of the Covenant. A Study of Israel from Moses to the Monarchy*, New York-Nashville, 1962, pp. 71ff.

of Yahweh in Canaan. It was most probably at Kadesh that Moses acted as priest and leader of this community.[1] Certainly in the preaching of Hosea the tradition of Israel's election in the desert is united to the theme of the deliverance of the exodus,[2] and, in the light of the prominence of the Kadesh community in the beginnings of Israel, it is reasonable to accept that both exodus and wilderness sojourn had long been associated together. They represent varying aspects of the one decisive series of events which gave birth to Israel.

The events of the exodus and wilderness sojourn both together pointed forward to the conquest of Canaan as the goal of Yahweh's actions towards Israel, since some such action was essential to account for the transition from Kadesh into Canaan. Exodus, wilderness-sojourn and conquest all belonged to the same nexus of events, which formed the foundation story of Israel's history, and which were understood by the prophets as ordained by Yahweh because he had chosen Israel to be his people. It is clear, in consequence, that reference to such a desert origin of Israel does not refer to any kind of 'nomadic tradition' about the nation's past, or of any of the tribes of which the nation was comprised. The ancestors of Israel were not true nomads, but mainly lived a half-settled, semi-nomadic existence. Many had already advanced more than half-way towards the Canaanite pattern of settled life before they became members of Israel. Nomadism never provided Israel with its ideal of orthodoxy, nor did it represent for them an especially sacred way of life.[3]

This appeal back to the exodus complex of events, with its theological interpretation as Yahweh's election of Israel to be his people, plainly holds a fundamental place for Amos and Hosea. Their whole understanding of Yahweh is coloured by it, and their

[1] M. L. Newman, *op. cit.*, pp. 83ff.; E. Osswald, 'Mose', *RGG*[3] IV, cols. 1151ff.; *Das Bild des Mose in der kritischen alttestamentlichen Wissenschaft seit J. Wellhausen*, Berlin, 1962, pp. 339f.

[2] Cf. E. Rohland, *Die Bedeutung der Erwählungstraditionen Israels für die Eschatologie der alttestamentlichen Propheten*, Dissertation, Heidelberg, 1956, pp. 31ff.

[3] Contra J. W. Flight, 'The Nomadic Idea and Ideal in the Old Testament', *JBL* 42, 1923, pp. 158ff. Cf. R. de Vaux, *Ancient Israel*, London, 1961, p. 14, 'Nomadism itself is not the ideal; rather, it is that purity of religious life and that faithfulness to the Covenant, which was associated in Israel's mind with its former life in the desert.'

entire message to Israel presupposed the fact that the people whom they addressed had been chosen by Yahweh. This same appeal to the exodus tradition was of fundamental significance also for Jeremiah and Ezekiel. It is all the more surprising therefore that there is scarcely any reference at all to the exodus in the two great Judean prophets, Isaiah and Micah, who were active towards the close of the eighth century.

In these prophets, instead of the appeal to the special election of Israel at the exodus, we find the whole understanding of Yahweh dominated by the distinctive cult-traditions of Jerusalem, and by a concern with the promises of Yahweh to the Davidic dynasty. Already Amos had made some use of these traditions,[1] but in these prophets they are given a greater prominence. Isaiah shows himself to be especially the prophet of Mount Zion, and, although he could use this election tradition as a motive to establish the people's unfaithfulness,[2] he saw in Yahweh's presence in Jerusalem the hope for the future of Israel and all nations.[3] There is a remarkable ambivalence in the preaching of Isaiah, therefore, in which the proclamation of judgment upon sinful Jerusalem is accompanied by belief in the manifestation there of Yahweh's power and victory over the nations.[4] In the light of the hopes

[1] Amos 1.2; 9.11–12. Both of these allusions to the Zion traditions in Amos have frequently been regarded by scholars as the result of editorial expansion and revision of the text. In view of the Southern origin of Amos (from Tekoa), it seems very probable that he did share much of the distinctive religious outlook and ideology of Jerusalem. Although Amos 1.2 may possibly be the work of a later editor, the promise of the restoration of the Davidic greatness (Amos 9.11–12) has a good claim to be an authentic utterance of the prophet. In Hos. 3.5 there is a reference to the David tradition, which must be regarded as a gloss, which was introduced into the collection of Hosea's prophecies at a time when they were brought south, and reapplied to Judah. So H. W. Wolff, *Hosea* (BKAT), Neukirchen, 1961, pp. 70, 79.

[2] Isa. 1.21–26.

[3] Isa. 2.2–4. This oracle is also found in Micah 4.1–4, but its authorship is more probably to be ascribed to Isaiah than to Micah. It is a prophetic recasting of many of the themes of the cult-traditions of Jerusalem, so that much of the language is traditional. Cf. G. von Rad, 'Die Stadt auf dem Berge', *Ges. Stud.z.A.T.*, Munich, 1958, pp. 214ff.; H. Wildberger, 'Die Völkerwallfahrt zum Zion. Jes. ii: 1–5', *VT* 7, 1957, pp. 62ff.

[4] That the preaching of Isaiah contained initially some expectation of a restoration of Israel after the destruction is argued by J. Bright, 'Isaiah', *Peake's Commentary on the Bible*, rev. ed. 1962, p. 490. In opposition to this view T. C. Vriezen, 'Essentials of the Theology of Isaiah', *Israel's Prophetic*

engendered by belief in Yahweh's presence on Mount Zion, promising security and prosperity for Yahweh's people, and the defeat of hostile nations who attacked them,[1] Isaiah foretold that Yahweh himself would fight for Israel from Mount Zion.[2] Just how this hope of Yahweh's triumph over Judah's enemies was reconciled with the proclamation of judgment upon Jerusalem is not clear.[3] In the traditions about Isaiah from the time of the Assyrian invasion under Sennacherib (701 BC), Isaiah is shown as the champion of the belief in Yahweh's presence which is the guarantee of Jerusalem's protection.[4] In Micah we find that this belief in Jerusalem's inviolability, because it was Yahweh's dwelling-place, was regarded as a false faith, which had become divorced from any sense of Israel's moral obligations to the covenant with Yahweh. Micah opposed it and foretold that Jerusalem would be destroyed.[5] This was a warning that Yahweh was about to end his particular relationship with his people, since it meant an end to the election of Mount Zion, on which the whole religious basis of the State of Judah rested.

In both Isaiah and Micah we find also a prominent use of the tradition of a covenant between Yahweh and the house of David. Both prophets, in recognizing the faithlessness of the current occupants of the throne of Judah, pointed beyond the coming destruction to a time when Yahweh would begin again, and would raise up a true heir to David. In those days the expectations of

---

Heritage, ed. Anderson and Harrelson, pp. 133ff., argues that Isaiah initially expected the total judgment of Jerusalem and Judah.

[1] E.g. Pss. 46, 48, 76. For the mythological background of this tradition see J. H. Hayes, 'The Tradition of Zion's Inviolability', *JBL* 82, 1963, pp. 419ff.

[2] Isa. 8.9f.; 14.32; 17.12–14; 28.14–18; 29.5–8. Cf. J. Pedersen, *Israel* III–IV, Copenhagen, 1940, pp. 551ff., who argues that Isaiah's message has been deeply influenced by the temple and the traditional Zion ideology. This is denied by T. C. Vriezen, *Israel's Prophetic Heritage*, pp. 128ff.

[3] In Isa. 29.1–4 a threat against Jerusalem is followed by a promise of deliverance (29.5ff.).

[4] Isa. 36–37. The historical nucleus of these appendices to the book of Isaiah's prophecies is uncertain, but they undoubtedly represent authentically the attitude of the great prophet to Jerusalem. Cf. O. Eissfeldt, *Einleitung in das Alte Testament* (2 Aufl.), Tübingen, 1956, pp. 396f. (Engl., *Introduction to the Old Testament*, Oxford, 1965.)

[5] Micah 3.9–12.

peace and happiness, contained in Yahweh's covenant-promises to David would be fulfilled.[1]

The prophetic collections of both Isaiah and Micah do contain references to the exodus, but their authenticity is contested.[2] In Jeremiah we find that the prophet is fully cognizant of the tradition of Israel's election in the exodus, and gives it a position of great emphasis,[3] but he is also aware of the popular beliefs concerning Jerusalem and the Davidic house. Israel's special position before Yahweh was a result of his grace, shown to it by the election of Israel at the exodus. It was against this election-grace that the people had rebelled ever since they had entered the land of Canaan. The time of the election in the wilderness is particularly regarded as the age of Yahweh's special revelation to the people.[4] Yet alongside of this exodus tradition, we find also promises derived from the belief in Yahweh's covenant with the house of David.[5] The distinctive cult-tradition of Jerusalem was opposed by Jeremiah, as by Micah before him, because it had led to a false and immoral trust in the actual building of the temple.[6] In Jeremiah's

[1] Isa. 7.14ff.; 8.23–9.6 (EVV 9.1–7); 11.1–9; Micah 5.1–5 (EVV 2–6). The Immanuel prophecy is well known for its difficulties of interpretation, but most probably the prophet is here foretelling the birth of a royal heir, through whom the promises to the Davidic dynasty would find fulfilment. So S. Mowinckel, *He That Cometh*, Oxford, 1956, pp. 110ff.; E. Hammershaimb, 'The Immanuel Sign', *StTh* 8, 1949, pp. 124ff.; C. R. North, 'Immanuel', *IDB* II, pp. 685bff. The alternative view that the Immanuel child is that of the prophet is argued by J. J. Stamm, 'La prophétie d'Emmanuel', *RHPR* 23, 1943, pp. 1ff.; 'Neuere Arbeiten zum Immanuel-Problem', *ZAW* 68, 1956, pp. 46ff.; 'Die Immanuel Weissagung. Ein Gespräch mit E. Hammershaimb', *VT* 4, 1954, pp. 20ff.; N. K. Gottwald, 'Immanuel as the Prophet's Son', *VT* 8, 1958, pp. 36ff.

L. Köhler, 'Zum Verständnis von Jes.7.14', *ZAW* 67, 1955, pp. 48ff., has argued that the reference to 'the young woman' (Heb. *hāʿalmā*) is to be taken collectively for 'young women'. Cf. also G. Fohrer, 'Zu Jes.7.14 im Zusammenhang von Jes.7.10–22', *ZAW* 68, 1956, pp. 54ff.

[2] Isa. 4.2–6; 10.24–26; 11.16; Micah 6.4. The Isaiah references are regarded as unauthentic by E. Rohland, *Die Bedeutung der Erwählungstraditionen Israels für die Eschatologie der alttestamentlichen Propheten*, pp. 113f., 116f. Cf. also G. von Rad, *Theologie des A.T.* II, pp. 175f., 178. For Micah 6.4 see E. Rohland, *op. cit.*, pp. 59f. note, but cf. also A. Weiser, *Kleinen Propheten* I (ATD 24), pp. 230f., 277ff. W. Beyerlin, *Die Kulttraditionen Israels in der Verkündigung des Propheten Micha* (FRLANT 72), Göttingen, 1959, pp. 29ff., defends the genuineness of the references to the exodus tradition in Micah.

[3] Jer. 2.5–7; 7.21f.; 16.14f.; 23.7f.; 31.31–34.

[4] Cf. Jer. 7.22.

[5] Jer. 23.5f.; cf. 22.30.

[6] Jer. 7.1–15; 26.1–24.

contemporary, Zephaniah, we find themes drawn from the Zion-tradition being used to express Yahweh's purposes for his people.[1]

Ezekiel, like Jeremiah, shows a familiarity with both the exodus and Zion traditions. Both were clearly known to the prophet, and both furnished him with material for his understanding of Yahweh and his purposes with Israel. The exodus tradition, especially, is used in a way which shows that Ezekiel regarded it as determinative of Israel's position before Yahweh.[2] The indictment against Israel is that they have been unceasingly disloyal to the God who called them by his grace. Even at the moment of their election they had rebelled against Yahweh.[3] There is no doubt that Ezekiel here shows that for him the election of Israel at the exodus was the fundamental fact about its existence. Yet he also made use of the traditions of a covenant between Yahweh and David, with its promises for the Davidic dynasty.[4] The Programme of Reconstruction, which is appended to Ezekiel's prophecies (chs. 40–48), shows many features of the Zion cult-traditions.

The use by the prophets of these traditions about Israel's origin, with their particular stress on the exodus, and on the covenant between Yahweh and the house of David, shows that the knowledge of God, which the prophets had, was guided by the particular traditions which they inherited.[5] Their understanding of who Yahweh was, and what Israel was meant to be, owed much to the historical and cultic traditions which had been preserved in the nation. In the consciousness of the prophet the awareness of direct communion with Yahweh was fed and nourished

[1] Zeph. 3.6–8, 9–10, 11–13.
[2] Ezek. 20.1–44.
[3] Ezek. 20.5–8.
[4] Ezek. 34.23–30; 37.15–28; cf. 17.23–24.
[5] The importance of the religious traditions of Yahwism for an understanding of the prophets was argued by S. Mowinckel, *Die Erkenntis Gottes bei den alttestamentlichen Profeten*, pp. 7ff., 32. Cf. also G. Henton Davies, 'The Yahwistic Tradition in the Eighth-century Prophets', *Studies in Old Testament Prophecy*, ed. H. H. Rowley, Edinburgh, 1946, pp. 37ff.; E. Rohland, *op. cit.*, pp. 20ff.; W. Beyerlin, *Die Kulttraditionen Israels in der Verkündigung des Propheten Micha, passim.* A more critical assessment of the importance of such traditions is made by G. Fohrer, 'Tradition und Interpretation im A.T.', *ZAW* 73, 1961, pp. 1ff., and in 'Remarks on Modern Interpretation of the Prophets', *JBL* 80, 1961, pp. 313f. Fohrer argues that, although the prophets utilized older traditions of Israel, they were not bound by them, and interpreted them in wholly new ways.

by the knowledge that was provided by these traditions. Their prophetic inspiration did not preclude their dependence upon such an inherited form of knowledge, but in every way presupposed it.

It is apparent that whilst the David-covenant tradition was exclusively handed on in a Judean milieu, and only appears in Southern prophets, it is not true that the exodus tradition was exclusive to North Israelite prophets.[1] Amos, Jeremiah and Ezekiel were all Southern prophets, and yet they show a considerable familiarity with both the exodus and David traditions. This is all the more remarkable when we bear in mind that Amos stands right at the beginning of the line of the canonical prophets. If the two traditions are regarded as only having been related at a late date,[2] then Amos stands out as an exception for the eighth century.[3] We must enquire then how the election of the exodus was related to the belief in Yahweh's election of Mount Zion and his covenant with David. Before we can do this satisfactorily we must look more closely at the tradition of the exodus. What really did this contain?

It has been argued by several scholars in recent years that the original tradition of the exodus contained no reference to a covenant on Mount Sinai, which was believed to have been introduced at a later stage.[4] Thus the theme of the exodus-election has

[1] Attention was particularly drawn to the parallel traditions of the Sinai covenant in Northern Israel, and the David covenant in Judah, by L. Rost, 'Davidsbund und Sinaibund', *TLZ* 72, 1947, cols. 129ff. Rost argued that these represented two parallel branches of tradition, which were linked together in Jerusalem at the time of the reformation of Josiah in 621 BC.

[2] Cf. E. Rohland, *op. cit.*, pp. 20ff., 269; G. von Rad, *Old Testament Theology* I, pp. 306ff., *Theologie des A.T.* II, pp. 203, 230.

[3] It must be borne in mind that although Amos was from the Southern Kingdom he prophesied in a Northern sanctuary, Bethel. See p. 49 above for the probable genuineness of the Zion-David tradition in Amos.

[4] The separation of the Sinai-covenant tradition from its context in the narratives of the exodus and desert wandering was proposed by S. Mowinckel, *Le décalogue*, Paris, 1927, pp. 114ff., on the grounds that the real origin of the Sinai-covenant story can be traced to a cultic celebration in Jerusalem. This was followed by G. von Rad, 'Das formgeschichtliche Problem des Hexateuch', *Ges. Stud.z.A.T.*, pp. 15ff., who traced the cultic basis of the Sinai-covenant story to a celebration of the Feast of Tabernacles in Shechem. Cf. also H. Wildberger, *Jahwes Eigentumsvolk* (ATANT 37), Zürich, 1960, pp. 40ff. Wildberger endeavours to separate out the pericope Ex. 19.3b–8 as an election tradition, and argues that this was at one time separate from the Sinai tradition. The election tradition he then locates at Gilgal and relates it to a celebration of the Feast of Unleavened Bread (*op. cit.*, pp. 55 ff.).

been separated from the idea of a covenant between Yahweh and Israel. This has been thought to find support in the extreme paucity of direct references to a covenant in the prophets before Jeremiah.[1] A full examination of this thesis, that the exodus tradition was at one time quite separate from the tradition of a covenant made on Mount Sinai, has been undertaken by W. Beyerlin,[2] and it would be superfluous to reiterate his detailed arguments. It will suffice to present his major conclusion, which is that the tradition of the exodus belongs essentially to the covenant on Mount Sinai.[3] The exodus points forward to the covenant as the goal of Yahweh's intervention on behalf of the oppressed Hebrews in Egypt, and the essential presupposition of the covenant is an act of grace on Yahweh's part. Election, through an act of deliverance, and the covenant, which defined the obligations of those who had received this salvation of Yahweh, belong inseparably together. Thus a tradition of history, recalling the events of the deliverance, and a tradition of law, setting out the obligations of those who had been elected, were both essential to the tradition of the covenant.

The idea of election demands a goal of some kind, which defines the meaning and purpose of that election. In other words it must lead to belief in some kind of special relationship between those who are elect, and he who elects them. Whether the term 'covenant' (Heb. *běrīth*) was used from the beginning to describe this relationship is only of secondary importance, although it is not impossible that this was the term used.[4] We must argue also that

1 As a reference to a divine covenant it is found only in Hos. 6.7 and 8.1 among the eighth-century prophets. For the use of the term compare also Amos 1.9; Hos. 2.20 (EVV 18); 10.4; 12.2 (EVV 1); Isa. 28.15, 18. Hos. 6.7 is frequently rejected as a corruption of the original text, and R. Kraetschmar, *Die Bundesvorstellung im Alten Testament in ihrer geschichtlichen Entwickelung*, Marburg, 1896, pp. 105ff., denies that Hosea referred to a divine covenant at all. But cf. H. W. Wolff, *Hosea*, pp. 154, 176f.

2 W. Beyerlin, *Herkunft und Geschichte der ältesten Sinaitraditionen*.

3 Cf. also W. Beyerlin, *Die Kulttraditionen Israels in der Verkündigung des Propheten Micha*, p. 65; A. Weiser, *Introduction to the Old Testament*, pp. 83ff.; N. W. Porteous, 'Actualization and the Prophetic Criticism of the Cult', *Tradition und Situation. Studien zur alttestamentlichen Prophetie*, ed. Würthwein and Kaiser, p. 95.

4 G. E. Mendenhall, 'Covenant', *IDB* I, p. 716a, argues on the basis of the paucity of direct references to a covenant between Yahweh and Israel in the earliest sections of the Old Testament that at first the relationship was not called a covenant. He suggests that it may have been called 'the ten words', or

the covenant of Sinai would have been effete and powerless had it not taken its origin in an act of divine grace, which brought Israel into its privileged position, and which placed an obligation upon it. This is especially true if the near-eastern suzerainty treaties provide any kind of useful parallel to the form of the Mosaic covenant. A historical prologue, setting out the events which led up to the conclusion of the covenant, was a constitutive part of the covenant document. This is very similar in form to the historical prologue of the Decalogue (Ex. 20.2), which relates the exodus to the Sinai-covenant law. That the connexion of the exodus with the covenant of Sinai is to be found in a single series of historical events is far more credible than that two unrelated themes have subsequently been joined together in a way which has such tremendous consequences for theology. We may confidently claim, therefore, that when the pre-exilic prophets referred to the events of the exodus, and of Israel's desert origin, they were referring to the fact that Israel was a covenant people, and were appealing to the fact of the divine grace which had originated that covenant. The prophetic appeal to the election of Israel was an appeal to the covenant. In this connexion the fact that the term 'covenant' is seldom used in the pre-exilic prophets, prior to Jeremiah, is no objection. It would have served the purpose of the prophets but little to have repeated the catchword 'covenant'. They placed their emphasis upon the grace which had brought the covenant into being, rather than upon a term which covered a wide variety of agreements, and which could so easily have been construed by their hearers as a slogan of national security.[1]

This covenant tradition, with its twofold themes of the divine grace revealed in Israel's election, and of the law, by which Israel was to attest its obedience to Yahweh, formed what Hosea in particular described as the knowledge of God.[2] This knowledge of

---

'the testimony' (Heb. *hā'ēdhūth*); cf. Ex. 31.18. He points out that in the case of 'testimony' the cognate Akkadian and Aramaic words were in common use for 'covenant'.

[1] Cf. W. Eichrodt, *Theology of the Old Testament* I, London, 1961, p. 374, and G. E. Wright, 'The Faith of Israel', *Interpreter's Bible* I, New York-Nashville, 1951, p. 357a.

[2] H. W. Wolff, ' "Wissen um Gott" bei Hosea als Urform von Theologie', *EvTh* 12, 1952-3, pp. 545ff. Cf. also J. L. McKenzie, 'Knowledge of God in Hosea', *JBL* 74, 1955, pp. 22ff., who especially refers such knowledge to an acquaintance with traditional Hebrew morality.

God was not a subjective experience of communion with him, but contained positive and objective traditions of history and law, which defined the nature and meaning of the covenant. Of course such objective knowledge was designed to lead to the experience of communion with Yahweh, but its character, in the form of historical and legal tradition, was intended to guard Israel against apostasy and disobedience.

We must ask then how this Sinai-covenant tradition was related to the particular Jerusalem-Judean traditions which centred on Mount Zion and the house of David. In order to clarify this relationship we must investigate more closely the content and significance of the Jerusalem traditions. These comprised two major themes: Yahweh has chosen Mount Zion to be his dwelling-place, and reveals himself there to all nations; secondly Yahweh has chosen David, and his dynasty, to rule over Israel. This second theme is presented in the form of a covenant between Yahweh and the house of David,[1] and we must enquire how this covenant was related to the belief in the election of Mount Zion. Arguments have been presented by some scholars to show that the theme of the election of Mount Zion was originally quite distinct from the tradition of a covenant with David.[2] Whether this was indeed so can only become apparent by a study of the nature of this Davidic covenant.

The origin of the idea of such a covenant between Yahweh and the house of David is found in the prophecy of Nathan recorded in II Samuel ch. 7. This oracle gives an account of how this covenant originated, and what it promised.[3] David, after securing

---

[1] II Sam. 7; Pss. 21.8 (EVV 7); 89.25, 29, 34f. (EVV 24, 28, 33f.); 132.11–12; Isa. 55.3.

[2] E. Rohland, *op. cit.*, pp. 20, 122f., 255; G. von Rad, *Theologie des A.T.* II, pp. 179, 184.

[3] The original text of the oracle, before the addition of certain expansive notes, is to be found in verses 1–7, 11b, 16, 18–21, 25–29. So L. Rost, *Die Überlieferung von der Thronnachfolge Davids* (BWANT III:6), Stuttgart, 1926, pp. 47ff. The literature on Nathan's oracle is extensive, and besides the important work of L. Rost may be mentioned: S. Mowinckel, 'Natan forjettelsen 2 Sam. kap.7', *SEA* 12, 1948, pp. 204ff.; M. Noth, 'David und Israel in 2 Sam. 7', *Ges. Stud.z.A.T.* (2 Aufl.), 1960, pp. 334ff.; M. Simon, 'La prophétie de Nathan et le Temple (Remarques sur II Sam. 7)', *RHPR* 32, 1952, pp. 41ff.; H. J. Kraus, *Die Königsherrschaft Gottes im Alten Testament*, Tübingen, 1951, pp. 35ff., 52ff., 92ff.; *Gottesdienst in Israel* (2 Aufl.), Munich, 1962, pp. 212ff.; S. Herrmann, 'Die Königsnovelle in Ägypten und Israel', *Wissen-*

peace in his kingdom, desired to build a temple as a permanent resting-place for the ark. Yahweh, through the mouth of Nathan, the court-prophet, refused his permission to do so, and promised that instead of David building a house (temple) for Yahweh, Yahweh would build a house (dynasty) for David. Thus, woven into the basic structure of the prophecy is a correlation between David's desire to build a temple, and the promise of Yahweh's support for the Davidic dynasty. Attempts have been made, on literary grounds, to separate out the promise to David and his sons (vv. 11b and 16) as the original nucleus of the prophecy.[1] Even if this is justified, the embedding of this promise in its context of a concern for the building of a temple must have taken place at a very early stage. Thus, in its basic form, Nathan's oracle is concerned with the question of Yahweh's dwelling-place in Jerusalem, as well as with the divine right of David and his sons to rule over Israel. This connexion between the desire for a temple, and the promise to David's house, is not a superficial literary allusion, based on the different meanings of 'house' (Heb. *bayith*)[2] in verses 5, 6, 7, 11b, 16, but is rooted in the very purpose of a temple. Temples in the ancient near east were very closely linked to the royal thrones of the earthly rulers, and gave expression to the belief in the sacral authority of the earthly ruler as the vice-regent of the deity.[3] When eventually a temple was built by Solomon, David's successor, it was certainly used as a means to express the

---

schaftliche Zeitschrift, Leipzig 3, 1953–4, pp. 57ff.; E. Kutsch, 'Die Dynastie von Gottes Gnaden. Probleme der Nathanweissagung in 2 Sam. 7', *ZTK* 58, 1961, pp. 137ff.; G. W. Ahlström, 'Der Prophet Nathan und der Tempelbau', *VT* 11, 1961, pp. 113ff.; A. Caquot, 'La prophétie de Nathan et ses échos lyriques', *Congress Volume, Bonn 1962* (SVT 9), Leiden, 1963, pp. 213ff.; J. Schreiner, *Sion-Jerusalem. Jahwes Königsitz* (SANT 7), Munich, 1963, pp. 73ff.

[1] L. Rost, *Die Überlieferung von der Thronnachfolge Davids*, p. 62; but E. Kutsch, *art. cit.*, pp. 144ff., argues that the original kernel of the oracle is to be found in verse 11b only, and that substantially we must regard the prophecy, apart from the recognized additions, as a unity.

[2] This is argued by L. Rost, p. 71, who regards the verses expressing Yahweh's refusal of a temple as having been combined later with the original prophecy of a divinely established dynasty for David by means of the catchword 'house'.

[3] K. Möhlenbrink, *Der Tempel Salomos* (BWANT IV:7), Stuttgart, 1932, pp. 48ff., 79.

belief in Yahweh's support for Solomon's throne.[1] It is apparent at every point that Nathan's oracle was an utterance fraught with political consequences of the most far-reaching kind. The promise that David's throne would be established by Yahweh, both for David himself and for his sons, was not only a personal aggrandizement for the king, but conveyed an expression of how Yahweh himself willed that his people Israel should be governed. Nathan's oracle thus represents a divinely given charter for the monarchical State which David introduced into Israel, and which Solomon carried through to the completion of its organization. This monarchical State was believed to have been set under the hand of David and his sons by Yahweh.

The connexion of this divine election of David, which is revealed in Nathan's oracle, with the building of a temple, was also full of political overtones. The temple that was eventually built by Solomon, and which must certainly be considered in relation to the building which David intended to erect, was a State sanctuary, conceived as the supreme Yahweh sanctuary of Israel.[2] As a royal shrine it was intended to be the centre of divinely given blessing for all the nations. In pursuance of this aim Solomon housed the ancient ark there, in accord with the original intention of David (II Sam. 7.2). This ark, which had become associated with Yahweh's cherubim-throne,[3] was the central cult-object of the old

[1] This is shown by the recollection of Nathan's prophecy at the dedication of the temple (I Kings 8.25–26). The free-standing pillars at the entrance to the temple were inscribed with what must have been dynastic oracles 'Jachin' and 'Boaz'. Cf. R. B. Y. Scott, 'The Pillars Jachin and Boaz', *JBL* 58, 1939, pp. 143ff., and in 'Jachin and Boaz', *IDB* II, pp. 780a–781a. The purpose of the pillars was apparently to give visible expression to the idea of the permanence of the royal dynasty. Cf. W. Kornfeld, 'Der Symbolismus der Tempelsäulen', *ZAW* 74, 1962, pp. 5off.

[2] It is misleading to regard the temple as no more than a private royal sanctuary, simply because it was attached to the royal palace. The whole ideology of the temple shows that it was concerned with the State and its welfare. It was no more private than the king himself could have been called a private person. See H. Vincent, 'Le caractère du Temple Salomonien', *Mélanges bibliques rédigés en l'honneur de André Robert*, Paris, 1957, pp. 137ff., and R. de Vaux, *Ancient Israel*, p. 320.

[3] The connexion of the ark with the idea of a divine cherubim-throne probably took place at Shiloh. Cf. O. Eissfeldt, 'Jahwe Zebaoth', *Miscellanea Academica Berolinensia*, Berlin, 1950, pp. 144f., and 'Silo und Jerusalem', *Volume du congrès, Strasbourg 1956* (SVT 4), Leiden, 1957, p. 146. Cf. also R. de Vaux, 'Les chérubins et l'arche d'alliance. Les sphinx gardiens et les

Yahweh amphictyony of the Israelite tribes. For David to have taken possession of it, and to have brought it to Jerusalem, was a political manoeuvre which greatly strengthened his hand in binding the associations of the old Yahweh covenant to the new situation created by his monarchical position in a territorially defined State. David sought to claim for his kingship, and the new political situation which he introduced, the sacral authority and traditions of the earlier covenant of the twelve-tribe federation.[1] In other words he sought to relate his kingdom to the divine promises revealed in the covenant made on Mount Sinai.[2]

It is also clear that the possession of the ark, and its eventual permanent home in the temple, were basic elements in the assertion of the divine election of Mount Zion. In fact it has been argued that the doctrine of the election of Mount Zion by Yahweh was nothing other than a particular way of expressing the claim of Jerusalem, and its temple on Mount Zion, to keep the ark, which had previously been the property of all the tribes.[3] This certainly was an important element, but it cannot be divorced from another relevant feature; the adoption by Israel of some of the earlier cult-traditions belonging to El-'Elyon, who had been the chief deity worshipped by the Jebusites in Jerusalem before

---

trônes divins dans l'ancien Orient', *MUSJ* 36, 1961, pp. 94, 119, 123, and in 'Arche d'alliance et Tente de Réunion', *À la rencontre de Dieu. Mémorial A. Gelin*, Le Puy-Lyon-Paris, 1961, p. 67.

[1] Cf. M. Noth, 'Jerusalem und die israelitische Tradition', *Ges. Stud.z.A.T.* (2 Aufl.), pp. 174ff.; 'David und Israel in 2 Sam. 7', *ibid.*, pp. 340ff.; *A History of Israel*, p. 191.

[2] M. L. Newman, *The People of the Covenant, passim,* sets out a finely detailed thesis arguing that from the days of the covenant community at Kadesh, there were two covenant traditions; a 'kingdom of priests' theology preserved in the northern tribes, and eventually crystallized in the E document, and a 'priestly-dynastic' theology of the covenant, preserved by the southern tribes, and eventually appearing in the J document. The latter covenant theology became dominant for David and his dynasty. Whilst many of the points adduced by Newman are extremely important, it is arguable that much of the 'priestly-dynastic' theology of J and the Davidic court entered Israel from the Jebusite El-'Elyon cult, and was anachronistically projected back by the Yahwist into the Sinai covenant. That features of sacral kingship ideology appear in the biblical portrait of Moses is argued by J. R. Porter, *Moses and Monarchy*, Oxford, 1963.

[3] H. J. Kraus, *Die Königsherrschaft Gottes im A.T.*, pp. 37, 43f.; *Gottesdienst in Israel* (2 Aufl.), pp. 213ff.

David's capture of the city.[1] These contained, among other features, belief in Mount Zion as a divine dwelling-place, and its identification with the sacral Mount Zaphon.[2] The sacred association of the mountain was very closely concerned with the divine ownership of the surrounding territory.[3] By adopting the belief that Mount Zion was a divine dwelling-place, and by remoulding this in a Yahwistic form to claim that Mount Zion had been chosen by Yahweh for his abode, David was making use of a religio-political doctrine which asserted administrative rights over Jerusalem, and which provided a religious authority for the Israelite State. The doctrine of the election of Mount Zion gave expression in Israel's faith to Yahweh's claim to sovereignty over Canaanite land, and was integrated into the earlier Yahwistic tradition by the bringing up of the ark into Jerusalem. Eventually this cult-object was given a permanent home in the temple there.

[1] A. R. Johnson, 'The Rôle of the King in the Jerusalem Cultus', *The Labyrinth*, ed. S. H. Hooke, London, 1935, pp. 81ff., 89, etc.; *Sacral Kingship in Ancient Israel*, Cardiff, 1955, esp. pp. 42ff.; H. Schmid, 'Jahwe und die Kulttraditionen von Jerusalem', *ZAW* 67, 1955, pp. 168ff.; J. Schreiner, *Sion-Jerusalem. Jahwes Königsitz*, pp. 19f.; H. S. Nyberg, 'Studien zum Religionskampf im Alten Testament', *ARW* 35, 1938, pp. 351ff., 357; E. Rohland, *op. cit.*, pp. 135ff.

[2] Cf. Ps. 48.3 (EVV 2). In the Ugaritic texts Mount Zaphon is exclusively the dwelling-place of Baal. O. Eissfeldt, *Baal Zaphon, Zeus Kasios und der Durchzug der Israeliten durchs Meer*, Halle, 1932, pp. 5ff.; 'Baal', *RGG*³ I, cols. 805f.; A. S. Kapelrud, *Baal in the Ras Shamra Texts*, Copenhagen, 1952, pp. 57ff. In Isa. 14.13–14 this mountain is connected with the deity 'Elyon.

[3] The Israelites identified El-'Elyon with Yahweh (Gen. 14.22). Since El-'Elyon was 'Creator/owner (Heb. *qōnēh*) of sky and land' (Gen. 14.19, 22), Yahweh's usurping of his position, and the taking over of his dwelling-place, implied Yahweh's rule over the land which had been the property of El-'Elyon. Cf. H. S. Nyberg, *art. cit.*, pp. 351ff. A certain elasticity is present in the Hebrew meaning of 'land' (Heb. *'ereṣ*), which means both the whole earth and also the local part of that earth (Canaan in this case). In the mythological background which lies behind the phrase, there was a deliberate identification of the land of Canaan with the whole cosmos, which was created and ruled by the god. See S. Mowinckel, *Religion und Kultus*, Göttingen, 1953, pp. 75f.; *The Psalms in Israel's Worship* I, p. 19.
  The holy mountain, which came to be regarded as the dwelling-place of Yahweh, was representative of the whole land belonging to him (Ps. 78.54; Ex. 15.17). Cf. H. J. Kraus, *Psalmen* I, p. 547, and see also H. Frankfort, *The Birth of Civilization in the Near East*, London, 1951, p. 54; *The Art and Architecture of the Ancient Orient*, London, 1954, p. 6; K. Galling, *Die Erwählungstraditionen Israels* (BZAW 48), Giessen, 1928, p. 4; S. Mowinckel, *The Psalms in Israel's Worship* I, p. 134. On the whole subject see my article 'Temple and Land: a Significant Aspect of Israel's Worship', *TGUOS* 19, 1963, pp. 16ff.

Thus we can in no way isolate the doctrine of Mount Zion's election from belief in Yahweh's choice of David as ruler over Israel, for both find their meaning and origin in the political events of David's reign. Neither can we separate the 'mythological' aspect of the doctrine (the sacred mountain) from its 'historical' side (the installation of the ark), for both belong together to the sacred ideology of the Israelite State, even though they ultimately go back to very different religious traditions.

It may be objected that in fact David never built a temple, and that it was his successor, Solomon, who did so. It requires to be explained, therefore, why Solomon should have done what it was prohibited to David to do, and why the temple was nevertheless associated with David as its cult-founder. It is apparent that even in Ancient Israel itself there existed a consciousness that doctrine and history did not wholly correspond at this point, for an editor has introduced into the text of Nathan's oracle a gloss to explain this (verse 13a).[1] This is, however, no valid objection against regarding the basis of the oracle as authentic, reflecting the actual circumstances of David's reign, and against our claim that a connexion existed between the election of David, and that of Mount Zion. The doctrine that Yahweh had chosen Mount Zion for his dwelling-place arose prior to the building of a temple, which was in fact a consequence of the doctrine. The concern for the ark, and for the refashioning of the Jebusite myth of a divine abode on Mount Zion in an Israelite form, were factors present in David's reign. It is perfectly intelligible, therefore, that he should have tried to give full expression to the belief in Yahweh's choice of Mount Zion by building a temple there. Such a temple would have served as a symbol of the divine pleasure at the new political situation, and of the permanence of the covenant between Yahweh and David. Nathan's objection to this temple was on the grounds that it conflicted with the old Israelite tradition of Yahweh's

[1] This verse is recognized by almost every commentator to be a gloss since it is at variance with the mention of a total rejection of any temple (II Sam. 7.5–7). Only S. Mowinckel, 'Natan forjettelsen 2 Sam. kap. 7', *SEA* 12, 1948, pp. 207 f., retains the verse and argues that it expresses the real point of the whole oracle. He argues that the prophecy does not express any ideological rejection of the temple, but is an aetiological reflection on a cultic institution, explaining why Solomon and not David built the temple. Mowinckel regards the whole prophecy of Nathan as a late prose fabrication, which arose out of earlier hymnic celebrations of Yahweh's choice of David.

dwelling in a tent.[1] Behind this we can discern the voicing of dissent against David's high-handed innovations in Israel's life. It is clear that opposition did exist against David's new régime, as the rebellions that took place show, and Nathan's prophecy shows how this affected the religious affairs of David's State. By the time of Solomon such opposition had been silenced, so that a temple could be built, and it is very possible that Nathan himself, who supported Solomon's claim to the throne (I Kings 1.8, 22ff., 32ff.) was advocating caution to David, rather than voicing his own deepest desires.[2] The whole prophecy, therefore, in its original form, acknowledges the connexion between the royal household and the divine house, and explains why David, who was the Jerusalem cult-founder, did not also build the temple. It therefore presumes a connexion between the idea of Yahweh's election of David and that of Mount Zion,[3] and shows how the covenant with David was rooted in the old Israelite tradition.

This rather detailed examination of Nathan's prophecy has been necessary, because it forms the basis of the belief in Yahweh's covenant with David, and it establishes two important points. These are, first, that the election of Mount Zion by Yahweh is a part of the tradition of the covenant with David, and secondly, that Yahweh's covenant with David was not unconnected with the earlier Israelite tradition which centred on the covenant on Mount Sinai. Rather the covenant of Sinai and the covenant with David represent two stages in the development of the Israelite religion, and they cannot be neatly divided out between the two States after the disruption.[4] Whilst the Northern Kingdom rejected the belief in a covenant between Yahweh and David, and

[1] It is not strictly true that the ark had always been kept in a tent, since a temple of some kind had housed it at Shiloh (I Sam. 1.9, 24; 3.3, 15).

[2] Cf. G. W. Ahlström, 'Der Prophet Nathan und der Tempelbau', *VT* 11, 1961, pp. 113ff., who goes so far as to argue that Nathan was not a reactionary Yahwist, but a Jebusite, whose interest in preventing David's building of a temple was motivated by a desire to prohibit the building of a sanctuary which would have rivalled the older El-'Elyon temple.

[3] This is shown by the connexion of the two in Pss. 78.67–72; 132.11–18. See also H. J. Kraus, *Die Königsherrschaft Gottes im Alten Testament*, pp. 43f., and frequently; *Psalmen* II, pp. 879ff.; *Gottesdienst in Israel* (2 Aufl.), pp. 214ff.; J. Schreiner, *Sion-Jerusalem. Jahwes Königsitz*, pp. 75ff., 103ff., 135; S. Mowinckel, *The Psalms in Israel's Worship* I, pp. 129f.

[4] Cf. A. H. J. Gunneweg, 'Sinaibund und Davidsbund', *VT* 10, 1960, pp. 335ff.; M. L. Newman, *op. cit.*, pp. 149ff.

denied the unique claims of Jerusalem in favour of the older Sinai tradition, it appears that in the Judean cult the memory of the Sinaitic covenant was not wholly absent.[1] Whilst there was a measure of incompatibility between the older amphictyony and the sacral kingship of the Davidic dynasty, with its State sanctuary, the latter was neither ignorant of, nor indifferent to the former. Rather the Davidic kings sought to present the earlier history of Israel as finding its goal in the election of David and Jerusalem. The kingship superseded the amphictyony, which had, in any case, ceased to be a political power, but it was not wholly able to suppress the memory of Moses and the covenant on Mount Sinai. It is not difficult to understand that in the court circles all emphasis was placed upon the David-Zion ideology, but in the popular religion of both the Southern and Northern Kingdoms the Sinai covenant was not forgotten.[2]

We cannot then regard the prophetic use of the ideas of the covenant with David as evidence of a tradition wholly separate from that of the Sinai covenant. It was rather a particular development in Judah of the earlier covenant tradition, which was rejected in Northern Israel at the time of the disruption under Jeroboam I. A relationship between the Sinai-covenant tradition and the tradition of a covenant with David goes back to David's own reign, and this is further confirmed by other evidence in the Old Testament. First of all the fact that the ark was brought up to Jerusalem, and kept there, inevitably carries with it the implication that David was seeking to unite the ideology of the tribal federation to that of the monarchy. The considerable differences between the two inevitably meant that much of the older tradition was forced into the background.

Secondly it is clear from the evidence of some psalms, which are most likely to have been associated with the Jerusalem Autumn Festival, that the temple cult contained allusions to the covenant on Mount Sinai. This is evident in Ps. 68.8–11, 18 (EVV 7–10, 17),

---

[1] M. L. Newman, *op. cit.*, p. 164 note, argues that there was no renewal of the Sinai covenant implied in the Autumn Festival in Jerusalem, but such a denial goes too far. Aspects of the Sinaitic covenant were certainly present in the Jerusalem cult. See S. Mowinckel, *The Psalms in Israel's Worship* I, pp. 155ff.; H. J. Kraus, *Die Königsherrschaft Gottes im A.T.*, pp. 45ff.

[2] Cf. V. Maag, 'MALKŪT JHWH', *Congress Volume, Oxford 1959* (SVT 7), Leiden, 1960, pp. 148ff.

which is undoubtedly a very ancient psalm, probably dating from the Davidic-Solomonic era.[1]

We may also adduce as a third point the evidence of two psalms: the Song of Miriam (Ex. 15.1–18), and Psalm 78, which particularly set forth the election of David and Mount Zion as the goal and climax of the exodus and conquest.[2] They show how, from the Jerusalem viewpoint, Yahweh's purpose for Israel found its fulfilment in the Davidic covenant, so that the sacral king was the legitimate heir of the old amphictyony. The Song of Miriam, which in view of its celebration of Yahweh as King (Ex. 15.18) may well have belonged to the liturgy of the Autumn Festival in Jerusalem, is generally recognized as very early, probably dating from a period no later than the end of Solomon's reign.[3] Psalm 78 is often placed later, and frequently claimed as post-deuteronomic, but has recently found defenders for a very much earlier date.[4]

Finally we may point out that the epic history of Israel's origins compiled by the Yahwist (J) was probably composed in Solomon's reign, and attaches the greatest importance to the events of the exodus, and to the making of the covenant on Mount Sinai. This was certainly a Judean composition, and its author in all probabi-

[1] Cf. S. Mowinckel, *Der achtundsechzigste Psalm*, Oslo, 1953, pp. 68ff., where the original composition of the psalm is claimed as pre-Davidic, and is thought to have undergone a subsequent Jerusalem revision. But cf. also S. Mowinckel, *The Psalms in Israel's Worship* I, pp. 125, 172ff.; II, pp. 80, 152ff., and W. F. Albright, 'A Catalogue of Early Hebrew Lyric Poems (Psalm 68)', *HUCA* 23, Part 1, 1950–1, pp. 1ff.

[2] Ex. 15.13–17; Ps. 78.54, 56–77.

[3] W. F. Albright, *The Archaeology of Palestine* (rev. ed.), 1960, p. 233, dates the psalm not later than the thirteenth century BC. F. M. Cross, and D. N. Freedman, 'The Song of Miriam', *JNES* 14, 1955, pp. 237ff., regard the psalm as having been composed in the twelfth to eleventh centuries, and written down in the tenth century BC. The clear allusion to Mount Zion, however, rules out a date earlier than the tenth century. Cf. S. Mowinckel, *The Psalms in Israel's Worship* I, pp. 126, 177; II, p. 247.

[4] For a post-deuteronomic date see R. Kittel, *Die Psalmen*, Leipzig, 1914, p. 293, and H. Junker, 'Die Entstehungszeit des Ps. 78 und des Deuteronomiums', *Biblica* 34, 1953, pp. 487ff. An earlier dating is defended by B. D. Eerdmans, *The Hebrew Book of Psalms* (OTS 4), Leiden, 1947, pp. 379ff. O. Eissfeldt, 'Das Lied Moses Deuteronomium 32, 1–43, und das Lehrgedicht Asaphs, Psalm 78 samt einer analyse der Umgebung des Mose-Liedes', *BSAW* 104-5, 1958, pp. 41ff., regards the psalm as having been composed before the disruption of the empire at Solomon's death, and thinks that Asaph, a contemporary of David, may have been its author. Cf. also A. Weiser, *The Psalms*, p. 540.

lity was to be found in the court circles of Solomon.[1] Our conclusion, therefore, is that the Southern (Judahite) tradition of
Yahwism, which focused on the election of Jerusalem and the
Davidic house, interpreted this as a legitimate development and
goal of the covenant made between Israel and Yahweh on Mount
Sinai. The ideas and hopes which were associated with Yahweh's
promises to David had as their indispensable presupposition the
covenant of Sinai. Whilst it is clear, therefore, that the religious
tradition of Judah contained ideas relating to Jerusalem and the
Davidic house which were rejected in the Northern Kingdom,
we may claim that it was neither ignorant of, nor indifferent to,
the earlier covenant tradition of Israel, which reached back to the
days of Moses. The Judean prophets Amos, Jeremiah and Ezekiel,
who all show a familiarity with both main currents of the Israelite
election traditions, were giving expression to basic features of the
religious faith of Judah, as it had been since the age of David.
Whilst the Deuteronomic reform of 621 BC undoubtedly gave a
greater emphasis to the Sinai tradition, and introduced considerable modifications and reinterpretations into the cult-tradition of
Jerusalem and its royal house, this was facilitated by the fact that
the memory of the Sinaitic covenant was already in the background of the religion of Judah.

We may summarize the results of this investigation into the
particular election traditions of Israel, to which the pre-exilic
prophets referred, by pointing to certain main features. The
election of Israel took place at the exodus and gave rise to the
making of a covenant between Yahweh and Israel on Mount
Sinai. In the age of David this covenant tradition was refashioned
and developed to form a divine authorization for the new State
which was created, with its own territorial and political claims.
Thus there was evolved the doctrine of the dual election of the

---

[1] The Yahwist presents Israel's history under the theme of divine promises
made to the patriarchs, the chief of whom is Abraham. The promises of
possession of the land of Canaan, of his descendants becoming a great nation
and of becoming a blessing for the nations were fulfilled in the existence of
the Davidic empire. The covenant with David was probably modelled in
part on the tradition of Yahweh's covenant with Abraham. (Cf. Gen. 12.3
with Ps. 72.17.) See G. E. Mendenhall, 'Covenant', *IDB* I, pp. 717bf. and
O. Kaiser, 'Traditionsgeschichtliche Untersuchung von Genesis 15', *ZAW*
70, 1958, p. 124. The Yahwist traces the fulfilment of the patriarchal promises
through the covenant of Sinai.

Davidic house to rule over Israel and of Mount Zion to be Yahweh's dwelling-place. After the disruption this Jerusalem-Davidic
tradition was rejected by the Northern Kingdom, and the primacy
of the Sinaitic covenant maintained. In Judah the central place was
given, in court circles at least, to the Davidic covenant, until the
reform of Josiah once again asserted the priority of the Mosaic
covenant. After this time aspects of both traditions became intermingled and interrelated. Thus whilst the Northern religious
tradition knew only the covenant of Sinai, the Southern tradition
related this in varying measure to a covenant between Yahweh and
the house of David.

Before we leave this survey of the use of the traditions of
Israel's election by the pre-exilic prophets we must give our attention to a further significant feature. This is the great paucity of
references in these prophets to the patriarchs, and the lack of any
insistence upon their share in the great scheme of Yahweh's purpose which gave life to Israel. K. Galling drew attention to this
fact in his study of the election traditions of Israel,[1] where he was
able to show that the pre-exilic prophets drew primarily upon the
theme of Israel's election at the exodus. It was only during and
after the exile that the patriarchs began to feature in Israelite
prophecy as the founders of the nation, and as the first to receive
the call of Yahweh.[2] Among the pre-exilic prophets it is only
Hosea who makes any considerable use of traditions about the
patriarchs.[3] The patriarchs, therefore, did not figure in the election
traditions of Israel until after the exile, when Yahweh's call of
Abraham, and the promises to Jacob, were looked upon as the
earliest beginnings of Yahweh's purpose with Israel. What explanation are we to offer for this? We cannot resort to the explanation
that Israel did not in fact know the stories of the patriarchs before
the exile since they figure in the earliest narratives of the pentateuch. We can assume, therefore, that pre-exilic Israel was generally familiar with stories about the patriarchs, even though the

[1] K. Galling, *Die Erwählungstraditionen Israels*, pp. 5ff.

[2] Isa. 51.2; 58.14; 63.16; 65.9; Ezek. 33.24.

[3] Hos. 12.4–5, 13 (EVV 3–4, 12). Cf. P. R. Ackroyd, 'Hosea and Jacob',
VT 13, 1963, pp. 245ff. References to the patriarchs by the pre-exilic prophets are also found in Isa. 29.22 (Abraham); Amos 7.16 (Isaac), and there
are a number of references to Israel as the House of Joseph, or the House of
Jacob.

canonical prophets, at least, did not regard them as playing a vital part in the growth of the Yahwistic tradition.

The reason for this must be that the stories of the patriarchs did not originally form a central part of the covenant tradition of Israel. They were at first only indirectly related to it. Whilst some parts of Israel identified the gods of the patriarchs with Yahweh,[1] it is apparent that there were also others who sharply distinguished them from the God of Israel.[2] For a long while no uniformity of attitude existed, but different sanctuaries presented the origins and claims of the Yahwistic religion in their own way.

When the patriarchal stories were taken up and used by the Yahwist and Elohist historians this literary development separated them from their original local setting in the cultic traditions of various sanctuaries. Indeed such a separation must already have been taking place when Israel's historians adopted them. During the period of the monarchy, therefore, Israel's cult maintained the exodus-Sinai tradition, which formed the main focus of the covenant faith, and the patriarchal traditions were secondary to this. This was certainly the case at Bethel, where Jeroboam took steps to infuse the cult with the exodus tradition (I Kings 12.28f.), even though a very noteworthy patriarchal legend already belonged to the shrine (Gen. 28).[3] It is very probable that such a proceeding also occurred at other shrines. The prophets were probably reflecting the attitude of the cult of Israel, therefore, in appealing to the exodus and Davidic election traditions, rather than to the patriarchs, whose memory was more widely preserved in popular folktales. At the time of the exile, when the Yahwistic

---

[1] Ex. 3.13–15; (E); 6.2 (P); cf. 34.5–7 (J). O. Eissfeldt, 'Jahwe, der Gott der Väter', *TLZ* 88, 1963, cols. 481ff., argues that the community at Kadesh identified Yahweh with the god of their ancestors, who had by this time been identified with the El god of Canaan. Cf. also J. P. Hyatt, 'Yahweh as the God of My Father', *VT* 5, 1955, pp. 130ff.

[2] Josh. 24.14; cf. Gen. 35.2ff. For this more critical attitude of Yahwism towards the patriarchal religion see C. Steuernagel, 'Jahwe und die Vätergötter', *G.Beer Festschrift*, Stuttgart, 1935.

[3] H. Wildberger, *Jahwes Eigentumsvolk*, p. 71, argues that the patriarchal traditions were preserved by other circles, and at other sanctuaries, than those which maintained the memory of the exodus and the Sinai covenant. We must remember, however, that traditions were not always bound to cult-sites, but were carried about by population changes. During the period of the monarchy, especially, single sanctuaries preserved traditions of the different stages of their religious development.

tradition was of necessity largely separated from its place in the cult, the stories of the patriarchs began to assume a more prominent place in Israel's faith and worship. The preaching of the pre-exilic prophets as a whole shows that the main focus of their understanding of Yahweh was on the traditions of the exodus and of Yahweh's choice of David. These were mutually related stages in the development of Israel's covenant faith.

IV

THE LAW IN THE PRE-EXILIC PROPHETS

OUR previous chapter has shown the immense importance attached by the pre-exilic prophets to the traditions of the covenant in Israel. The repeated allusions to the election of Israel at the exodus, and, in the Judean prophets, to the David-Zion traditions, bear witness to the determinative significance of Israel's covenant status as the people of Yahweh. The presupposition of all that the prophets have to say to Israel is the fact of Yahweh's gracious calling of the people out of servitude into the freedom of his service. The very basis of the accusations which the prophets raised against Israel, and their explanation of the coming judgment, was that Yahweh had imposed certain demands upon his people which they had not fulfilled. The covenant carried with it a standard of conduct towards Yahweh, and towards other members of the covenant, with a threat that failure to fulfil these demands would result in the divine judgment falling upon the offenders. The fact that the people as a whole was guilty of such disobedience and failure was, in the eyes of the prophets, the direct cause of Yahweh's wrath, and the reason for his intention to break off his covenant with Israel. The existence of a covenant implied of necessity the existence of a series of obligations into which the covenant members were contracted. This does not mean that the covenant was a contract of equal partners, since the prophets insisted that the election, which brought the covenant into being, was an act of Yahweh's grace, but it means nevertheless that the covenant was a two-sided relationship.[1] Israel was

[1] J. Begrich, 'Berit. Ein Beitrag zur Erfassung einer alttestamentlichen Denkform', *ZAW* 60, 1944, pp. 1ff., argued that the nature of a covenant was originally that of a gift made by a superior to an inferior. Begrich claimed that in his relationship the receiving partner remained completely passive (pp. 2f.). Subsequently such a notion of the covenant was modified into that of a contract between two partners, and the older covenant ceremonies tended to be read in this light. The idea of the covenant solely as a gift cannot be accepted in the light of the evidence of both the biblical and extra-biblical

summoned to respond to the mercies that had been shown to it by keeping the laws which Yahweh had given.[1] A standard of law, expressing Yahweh's demands and expectations of Israel, was fundamental to the existence of the covenant, and we have already seen that the threats and promises of the covenant, which were proclaimed in the cult, were directed towards obtaining obedience to this law.

An examination of Israel's law codes shows that they presuppose the fact of the covenant, and their aim and purpose is to maintain a standard of conduct which is consonant with membership of the covenant community.[2] As such they differ from State laws, where the authority lies in the State itself, and where the intention is to regulate behaviour in the interests of national security and order.

---

sources. See especially G. E. Mendenhall, 'Covenant Forms in Israelite Tradition', *BA* 17, 1954, pp. 50ff., and in *IDB* I, pp. 714a ff. Mendenhall points to the close similarities of form between the Moses-Sinai covenant tradition and the suzerainty treaties of the ancient near east, especially as they are known in Hittite sources. An excellent illustration of this kind of treaty is offered by D. J. Wiseman, 'The Vassal-treaties of Esarhaddon', *Iraq* 20, 1958, pp. 1ff. Cf. also W. Beyerlin, *Herkunft und Geschichte der ältesten Sinai-traditionen*, pp. 59ff.; K. Baltzer, *Das Bundesformular. Sein Ursprung und seine Verwendung im Alten Testament* (WMANT 4), Neukirchen, 1960, pp. 19ff.; 1959, pp. 347ff. Recently the element of promise contained in the existence of a covenant has been stressed by A. Jepsen, 'Berith. Ein Beitrag zur Theologie der Exilszeit', *Verbannung und Heimkehr*, ed. Kuschke, pp. 161ff. It is probable, however, that we should be careful to distinguish between promissory covenants and suzerainty covenants as does G. E. Mendenhall, 'Covenant', *IDB* I, p. 717a. The O.T. accounts of the covenants with Abraham and David are of the promissory type.

[1] See above p. 23. Covenants were of many kinds and it is erroneous to argue that the term *běrith* in itself implied anything about the status of the two partners. Nevertheless the suzerainty type of covenant offers an instructive parallel to the O.T. accounts of the Sinai covenant. In this case an element of demand, in the form of law, together with a threat for non-compliance with its terms, was very important. The law cannot be comprehended solely in terms of a gift of grace, since it also had a very threatening aspect. This is particularly pointed out by W. Zimmerli, 'Das Gesetz im Alten Testament', *Gottes Offenbarung. Gesammelte Aufsätze*, Munich, 1963, pp. 270ff.; *Das Gesetz und die Propheten. Zum Verständnis des Alten Testaments*, Göttingen, 1963, pp. 68ff. (Engl., *The Law and the Prophets*, New York, 1965), and his review of G. von Rad's *Old Testament Theology* in *VT* 13, 1963, p. 106.

[2] Cf. M. Noth, 'Die Gesetze im Pentateuch. Ihre Voraussetzungen und ihr Sinn', *Ges. Stud.z.A.T.*, pp. 32ff. The Book of the Covenant (Ex. 20.22–23.19) is the closest approximation to a State law, and is the least imbued with the distinctive Israelite covenant ethos of the O.T. law codes.

The institution of the covenant by Yahweh, from its inception, contained a basic code of law which expressed the obligations imposed upon each Israelite.[1] It is very much easier to assert the fact of the existence of such a code of law than it is to define precisely its nature and contents. Nevertheless this fact alone is of immense importance, since it establishes the antiquity of a basis of law in Israel, in which the sanction and authority was that of Yahweh himself. Israel, as Yahweh's people, were subject to a code of conduct which represented for them the will of their God. No reason exists for supposing that such laws were originally only concerned with cultic requirements, and the developed tradition is so categorical that this was not so, that we are safe in assuming that it was never otherwise. Yahweh's will embraced the whole of life, and his demands were directed at each individual Israelite, who was held responsible for their fulfilment so far as they concerned him.[2] Thus the Israelite faith in Yahweh had a very pronounced ethical character from its inception; a fact which is firmly attested by our sources. Morality for Israel was always closely woven into the fabric of its religion.

Since such a basis of law was to be made known to each Israelite, it needed to be briefly formulated and publicly declared on suitable occasions, when the community were present, or adequately represented. This quite certainly took place in the setting of the cult, and in particular on the occasion of the major Israelite festival, when the covenant itself was recalled and reaffirmed.[3] Israel's worship, therefore, had a very important function to fulfil in preserving the tradition of the covenant law, and in making it known to every Israelite. Law in Israel became in consequence a

[1] Cf. A. Alt, 'Die Ursprünge des israelitischen Rechts', *Kleine Schriften* I, pp. 328ff.; G. E. Mendenhall, 'Ancient Oriental and Biblical Law', *BA* 17, 1954, pp. 26ff.

[2] G. von Rad, *Old Testament Theology* I, pp. 191f., stresses that the 'thou' addressed in the Decalogue is Israel as a whole as well as the individual, since the individual did not stand in independence over against the group. But compare also G. E. Mendenhall, 'The Relation of the Individual to Political Society in Ancient Israel', *Biblical Studies in Memory of H. C. Alleman*, New York, 1960, pp. 100ff., for the importance of the individual's responsibility to the law in early Israel.

[3] Cf. Deut. 31.9–13, which commands the reading of the law at the Feast of Tabernacles every seventh year. The place of the laws in the cult is especially argued by A. Weiser, *The Psalms*, pp. 31f.; S. Mowinckel, *Le décalogue*, pp. 114ff.

special concern of the cult and its officials. Other kinds of law collections certainly existed in the form of handbooks for those who administered justice. These were the case laws, of which the Book of the Covenant, in the majority of its prescriptions, is the best example.[1] The cult-officials also began to develop manuals of procedure for the special duties which were of primary importance to their vocation.[2] Nevertheless the main basis of Israel's law was centred around the brief injunctions which were proclaimed in the covenant cult. Here the fundamental standard of conduct for Israel as a whole was defined and declared. These were the apodeictic laws, which were composed for public recital in the festival cult, and which Alt found to be the primary basis of laws which Israel brought with them into the land of Canaan.[3]

It has been suggested that the early amphictyonic organization of Israel contained the office of a 'law-speaker', who was responsible for the oversight of the covenant law.[4] He was both the

[1] A. Alt, 'Die Ursprünge des israelitischen Rechts', *Kleine Schriften* I, pp. 285ff.

[2] Cf. the Manual of Sacrifice in Lev. 1.1–5.26 (EVV 6.7), which contains prescriptions which have only been developed over a long period. See R. Rentdorff, *Die Gesetze in der Priesterschrift. Eine gattungsgeschichtliche Untersuchung* (FRLANT 62), Göttingen, 1954.

[3] A. Alt, 'Die Ursprünge des israelitischen Rechts', *Kleine Schriften* I, pp. 302ff. An examination of Alt's form-critical analysis is made by R. Kilian, 'Apodiktisches und kasuistisches Recht im Licht ägyptischer Analogien', *Biblische Zeitschrift* (NF) 7, 1963, pp. 185ff. It is doubtful whether Alt's claim that the apodeictic law was distinctively Israelite can be maintained. See, besides Kilian's article, G. E. Mendenhall, 'Ancient Oriental and Biblical Law', *BA* 17, 1954, pp. 29ff. E. Gerstenberger, *Wesen und Herkunft des sogenannten apodiktischen Rechts im Alten Testament*, Dissertation, Bonn, 1961, pp. 95ff., has argued that the origin of the apodeictic form of law was not in the cult, but in the clan ethic in which the tribal father prohibited actions detrimental to the group. Gerstenberger relates the apodeictic form closely to that of the early Wisdom teaching (pp. 100ff.). For a survey and criticism of Gerstenberger's thesis see H. Graf Reventlow, 'Kultisches Recht im Alten Testament', *ZTK* 60, 1963, pp. 267ff.

[4] Cf. A. Alt, 'Die Ursprünge des israelitischen Rechts', *Kleine Schriften* I, pp. 300f., who compares the references to the lists of minor judges in Judg. 10.1–5; 12.7–15, and suggests that they may have been entrusted with such a charge. Cf. also M. Noth, 'Das Amt des Richters Israels', *Bertholet Festschrift*, Tübingen, 1950, pp. 404ff., and H. J. Kraus, *Die prophetische Verkündigung des Rechts in Israel* (TS 51), Zollikon-Zürich, 1957. Kraus relates the task of such a law-speaker to that of the Mosaic office of prophet referred to in Deut. 18.15–20 (*op. cit.*, p. 18). This person was then the covenant mediator, and Kraus considers that the Levites later served as guardians of the office (p. 21). With the break-up of the amphictyonic circles the prophets endeavoured to actualize the old law traditions (pp. 30ff.).

guardian of the inherited law of the amphictyony, as well as the mediating authority for any new addition, or modification, to the existing law. If such an office may be regarded as having existed, then such a law-speaker carried out functions which were closely similar to those which tradition ascribes to Moses himself. The mediating role of the traditional founder of the covenant was handed on to a succession of followers who were entrusted with the oversight of Israel's law. Throughout the days of the amphictyony, therefore, a succession of officials may be thought to have taken responsibility for the proclamation of the demands of the covenant, and for the adherance of the several tribes to them. With the introduction of the monarchy it seems certain that such an office was taken over by the king, who could never have allowed the continued existence of a rival spokesman for all Israel.[1] It is possible that echoes of the tension between the amphictyonic law-speaker and the monarch are to be found in the rivalry between Samuel and Saul.

This brief study of the origins of Israel's law shows emphatically that the Israelite covenant itself proclaimed a code of law, and that such a law was fundamental to the standard of conduct expected of Israel. The basic purpose served by the existence and development of such a legal standard was to protect the covenant from infringements and violations which would jeopardize its continuance. Further, we have seen that the normal setting of this code of law was in the cult, where it was preserved and publicly declared.

When we come to enquire of the content and precise nature of this covenant law, we are directed immediately to consideration of the Ethical Decalogue of Ex. 20.2–17 (E). This is the code of law which is given the most prominent place in the account of the covenant ceremony on Mount Sinai, and it is apparent from its brief declaratory style that it was originally formulated for recitation in the cult.[2] These apodeictic laws were intended for oral

[1] H. J. Kraus, *Die prophetische Verkündigung des Rechts in Israel*, pp. 27ff., suggests the possibility that the old amphictyonic cult continued in separation from the State cult at such Northern shrines as Shechem and Gilgal.

[2] The claim that the Ethical Decalogue originated in the setting of the cult was strongly advocated by S. Mowinckel, *Le décalogue*, pp. 114ff., and has received wide acceptance since then. Cf. the studies of J. J. Stamm, *Der Dekalog im Lichte der neueren Forschung* (2 Aufl.), Bern, 1962, pp. 19ff.; and H. Graf Reventlow, *Gebot und Predigt im Dekalog*, Gütersloh, 1962, pp. 20ff.

communication in the cultic ceremonies, which reaffirmed the meaning and obligations of the covenant.[1] Their predominantly negative form ('Thou shalt not . . .') is a consequence of their purpose of preventing conduct prejudicial to maintenance of the covenant order. The main intention is to guard Israel against actions which could injure their relationship with Yahweh. As such they necessarily offer only a minimum standard of behaviour.[2] Such laws were in no way intended to provide a condition for the receiving of the covenant, but were indications how covenant loyalty to Yahweh was to be expressed. Obedience was not the presupposition of the covenant, but its consequence.[3]

The question remains whether the actual laws contained in the Decalogue of Ex. 20.2–17 represent the original demands made upon Israel on Mount Sinai. The short summary given above of the setting of the decalogic form shows that, whilst we are able to argue for the great antiquity of the presence of a code of laws in the covenant cult, it by no means follows that the original laws were identical with those in the present text of Exodus 20. It is certain that some expansion and elaboration has taken place of the quite brief prescriptions of the original ten words. Nevertheless strong arguments have been made for the Mosaic origin of this Decalogue in its original terse form.[4] In the Old Testament the use of a brief collection of ten, or twelve, laws is not restricted to

[1] The apodeictic form is entirely distinct from the casuistic form of the law manuals, and this difference of form probably reflects an origin in an entirely different situation. No claim can be made, on the basis of form alone, that one type must be older than the other, nor can any reason be shown how one type (the apodeictic) could arise by a natural chronological development out of the other (the casuistic) as C. F. Whitley argues, 'Covenant and Commandment in Israel', *JNES* 22, 1963, p. 44.

[2] We may compare in this regard the entrance *tôrôth* of Pss. 15 and 24.3–6, which sought to prevent unworthy Israelites from participating in the cult of Yahweh. On these entrance *tôrôth* see below pp. 82ff.

[3] Cf. E. Würthwein, 'Der Sinn des Gesetzes im Alten Testament', *ZTK* 55, 1958, pp. 266f.

[4] See most especially H. H. Rowley, 'Moses and the Decalogue', *Men of God*, London, 1963, pp. 1ff., and *The Faith of Israel*, p. 76. A late dating for the Ethical Decalogue is argued recently by C. F. Whitley, 'Covenant and Commandment in Israel', pp. 43ff. Whitley's arguments ignore, however, the demonstrations of the cultic background of the Sinai narrative, and the probable origin of the Decalogue in the cult. The ascription of law-codes to literary sources is of only limited value, since all such codes have undoubtedly undergone a long and continual process of development before reaching their present form. See E. Gerstenberger, *op. cit.*, p. 17.

Ex. 20.2–17. In Ex. 34.17–26 (J) we have the Yahwist's version
of the Sinai law, the so-called Ritual Decalogue.[1] This must also
be of great antiquity, though not necessarily greater than that of
the Ethical Decalogue. It represents another example of the kind
of decalogic formulation that was used in early Israel's cult, and
must represent a tradition deriving from a particular geographical
milieu.[2] The Book of the Covenant (Ex. 20.22–23.19), with its
manual of case laws, must itself be of very great age, and it owes a
great deal to Israel's borrowing from Canaanite legal practice.[3] It
betrays little of the distinctively Israelite national and religious
ethos, and for the most part deals simply with human relationships
and situations as such.

Although we must be content, therefore, to remain in some
uncertainty whether the present Decalogue of Ex. 20.2–17 is of
Mosaic origin, it is beyond doubt that it is a very early code of
laws, which was preserved in the covenant cult, and that its
prescriptions were intended to establish the norm of conduct
demanded of members of the covenant.[4] Some such brief code of
laws was in use in the Israelite community from its beginning,
setting forth the demands of Yahweh upon the people he had
redeemed. The community of Israel was very much aware of the
ethical nature of religious obedience, and its cult was closely tied
to the moral obligations which were the concern of every Israelite.
Before the rise of the canonical prophets in the eighth century
Israel had a long and deeply-embedded tradition of morality and
ethical religion. Yahweh was known as the God who watched over
the conduct of all who claimed to worship him, and the cult

---

[1] H. Kosmala, 'The So-called Ritual Decalogue', *Annual of the Swedish Theological Institute* I, Leiden, 1962, pp. 31ff., argues that this is not another decalogue, but an ancient feast calendar (verses 18–24), with an appendix (verses 25–26) of four additional injunctions relating to the Feast of Passover.

[2] For brief decalogues, or dodecalogues, we may notice also the Dodecalogue of Curses in Deut. 27.15–26, the Holiness Code Dodecalogue in Lev. 19.13–18, and perhaps a part of such a collection is also to be found in Ex. 21.12, 15–17.

[3] Cf. A. Alt, 'Die Ursprünge des israelitischen Rechts', *Kleine Schriften* I, pp. 291ff., who dates the Book of the Covenant between the period of the conquest and the formation of the State (p. 299).

[4] H. Graf Reventlow, *Gebot und Predigt im Dekalog*, pp. 20ff., argues that the Ethical Decalogue arose over a long period as the literary deposit deriving from the 'law-speaker' of the covenant cult.

itself was a vital instrument for the making known of his will.

The eighth-century prophets, therefore, were certainly not the first to introduce a strongly ethical note into the service of Yahweh, and they themselves were able to draw upon a long tradition of ethical teaching in Israel.[1] The accusations which Amos raised against the people for the injustice of their practices, and their neglect of the elementary standards of social righteousness, were authenticated by the demands of the covenant law which Israel knew. Amos was not the first to discover the ethical nature of religion, nor was he concerned to introduce a new morality into Israel. In passing sentence upon the sins of the people he was appealing to the fact that they had broken the covenant and flouted the law times without number. Such accusations would have carried no weight whatever if these demands for righteousness and justice were not already familiar to them. Behind Amos we must recognize the existence of a standard of covenant law, and its acceptance by the people as binding upon them.[2] Yahweh's intention to terminate his covenant with Israel was necessitated by the fact that Israel had already broken the covenant by a refusal to obey its laws. It was indeed not Yahweh, but Israel, which had brought the covenant to an end, and the impending judgment would only serve to make known this fact, and to punish the offenders.

An examination of the strictures of the prophets reveals that many of their strongest condemnations are for those whose responsibility it was to administer the law.[3] It was not Israel's not knowing the law, but its leaders' and judges' unwillingness to

---

[1] Cf. N. W. Porteous, 'The Basis of the Ethical Teaching of the Prophets', *Studies in Old Testament Prophecy*, ed. H. H. Rowley, pp. 143ff., and E. Hammershaimb, 'On the Ethics of the O.T. Prophets', *Congress Volume, Oxford 1959* (SVT 7), pp. 75ff.

[2] R. Bach, 'Gottesrecht und weltliches Recht in der Verkündigung des Propheten Amos', *Festschrift Günther Dehn*, Neukirchen, 1957, pp. 23ff., has endeavoured to show that Amos appeals to the apodeictic covenant law, rather than to the prescriptions of the casuistic laws, in his accusations against Israel. This is not a wholly convincing argument since Amos is concerned with the breakdown in the administration of justice, and points out breaches of case law (Amos 2.7, 8; cf. Ex. 21.9; 22.26). Nevertheless it is undoubtedly true that Amos's appeal to the law presupposes that that law represents the will of Yahweh in the covenant. The administration of justice, where the case laws belonged, was expected to further the aims of the covenant, and the case laws themselves were never a wholly secular affair.

[3] Amos 5.12; Hos. 5.1; Isa. 1.17, 23, 26; 5.23; 10.1–2; Micah 3.1, 9.

administer it fairly, that had led to such a lamentable disregard of righteousness. The judges are blamed, not because they do not possess an adequate code of just laws, but because they do not use them justly. As so often in the world's history, the law was good, but it was powerless without the will and integrity of strong men to enforce it. The anxiety of the prophets was to arouse the conscience of the nation to deal with those who had dishonoured their office by ignoring the very elements of justice. The prophets saw no need to teach a new code of law, or to institute a new kind of justice, but they saw every need to reveal plainly the corruption and dishonesty, which had robbed the citizens of Israel of the justice which was Yahweh's gift to them.

The covenant upheld its basis of law as an expression of the grace in which Yahweh had brought Israel out of Egypt and had taken them to be his people. The kindness which had been evident in the election of Israel had also given to them a standard of law by which to regulate their life, and to preserve the covenant from destruction. Yet, whilst it is apparent that the law was a gift of grace, it was not without a sterner aspect.[1] Even the Ethical Decalogue, which opens with a recollection of the divine favour shown to Israel (Ex. 20.2), contained also the threat of the wrath of Yahweh against disobedience (Ex. 20.5). The sanction of the covenant law was the holy will of Yahweh, which offered blessings for the obedient, but threatened a curse upon the disobedient. Amos, and the other great figures of pre-exilic prophecy, upheld the demands of the law with a rigour and effectiveness that Israel had not previously known. We have seen already, in our second chapter, the radical way in which Amos interpreted the threat of Yahweh's curse. From being a punishment for individual offenders within the covenant, Amos took it, and presented it as a sentence of death upon the whole of Israel. Before the curse of the law none in Israel could stand, for all had become guilty, and had to suffer the punishment decreed by Yahweh's wrath.[2] Far from

---

[1] Cf. W. Zimmerli, 'Das Gesetz im Alten Testament', *Gottes Offenbarung*, pp. 270ff. Zimmerli refers to Ex. 32.31ff. (E) and Num. 14.11ff. (JE) as evidence that even in the early pentateuchal sources the idea that the covenant could be threatened by disobedience was not absent. Cf. also his *Das Gesetz und die Propheten*, pp. 81ff.

[2] Cf. W. Zimmerli, 'Das Gesetz im Alten Testament', *Gottes Offenbarung*, pp. 270ff.

offering any kind of alternative moral standard to that demanded by the law, the prophets stressed as never before the absolutely binding nature of the law's demands. The covenant itself passed sentence upon Israel, and all that the prophets could do was to serve as Yahweh's messengers, announcing that the sentence would be carried out.

From the fact that we can discern the importance of the proclamation of the law in the covenant cult as an essential presupposition of the prophetic preaching, it has been argued that the prophetic presentation of Yahweh's lawsuit (German *Gerichtsrede*) was formulated upon a pattern developed in the cult.[1] Consequently it has been argued that the cult itself contained a kind of lawsuit, in which Yahweh raised accusations against offenders, and passed sentence upon them.[2] The speeches of Yahweh would be delivered in Yahweh's name by an authorized official.[3] This, however, depends on a very hypothetical reconstruction of some features of the cult, and, so far as the origin of the prophetic lawsuit-oracles is concerned, cannot be accepted. Whilst it is clear

[1] E. Würthwein, 'Der Ursprung der prophetischen Gerichtsrede', *ZTK* 49, 1952, pp. 1ff.

[2] E. Würthwein, *art. cit.*, pp. 11ff. Cf. also G. E. Wright, 'The Lawsuit of God: a Form-critical Study of Deuteronomy 32', *Israel's Prophetic Heritage*, ed. Anderson and Harrelson, pp. 26ff., who argues that the covenant lawsuit theme was a reformulation of the covenant renewal theme, which took place in North Israel among those who preserved the amphictyonic tradition. For the general pattern of the lawsuit in Israel see B. Gemser, 'The *Rîb*- or Controversy-Pattern in Hebrew Mentality', *Wisdom in Israel* (SVT 3), pp. 120ff. J. Harvey, 'Le "*Rîb*-pattern", requisitoire prophétique sur la rupture de l'alliance', *Biblica* 43, 1962, pp. 172ff., endeavours to derive the pattern of the prophetic lawsuit from the idea of the covenant as based on the form of near-eastern suzerainty treaties. This is unconvincing and lacks any positive evidence. It is much more probable that the prophets borrowed directly from the language of civil lawsuits and that the suzerainty demands also presupposed a generally similar basis of law.

[3] H. Graf Reventlow, whose work on Amos we have already noted, has made a thoroughgoing attempt to show that many forms of prophetic oracle were rooted in the cult. See *Das Amt des Propheten bei Amos*, pp. 89ff.; *Wächter über Israel. Ezechiel und seine Tradition* (BZAW 82), Berlin, 1962, *passim*; and *Liturgie und prophetische Ich bei Jeremia*, Gütersloh, 1963, *passim*. Graf Reventlow particularly relates the prophetic 'office' to that of the covenant 'law-speaker' of the old amphictyony, which, he believes, has provided the form for many of the prophetic utterances. See also his 'Prophetenamt und Mittleramt', *ZTK* 58, 1961, pp. 280ff., and also 'Grundfragen der alttestamentlichen Theologie im Lichte der neueren deutschen Forschung', *TZ* 17, 1961, pp. 96ff.

that the content of the accusations which the prophets levelled against Israel in the lawsuit was derived from the tradition of the covenant, the form itself was modelled upon the procedures developed in ordinary civil courts.[1] No specific cultic form of address was used by them, but rather a simple borrowing from the style of speeches used in the normal law processes of Israel, when no religious offence was in mind. Nevertheless the fundamental motif of all the accusations raised by the pre-exilic prophets of judgment is that Israel had broken the covenant which Yahweh had made with them. The evidence for this was furnished in abundance by the unrighteousness, immorality and wanton luxury which everywhere disfigured society. The task of the prophet was that of a messenger who announced the sentence which Yahweh had already passed on the offence.[2] The people of Israel were guilty of sinning against the covenant, and the punishment was banishment, and the end of their privileged relationship to Yahweh.

The attitude of the prophets to the law, and in particular the radical way in which they interpreted its demands, had led them to see a crisis in the history of the covenant. The smooth ordering of its life had been disrupted by the persistence and severity of Israel's sins. Against such sins the law uttered a curse, which admitted of no alleviation or escape. No alternative existed, therefore, but to declare that the covenant could not continue, and that Yahweh's wrath would fall, not on one or two irresponsible individuals, but upon the nation as a whole. The covenant necessitated its own dissolution by the judgment of the law which it contained.

The fact that the basis of morality which the prophets accepted was to be found in the covenant law is of immense importance. Had they taken their ethical standard from elsewhere, they could not have accused Israel of disloyalty to the covenant in the way

---

[1] Cf. H. E. von Waldow, *Der traditionsgeschichtliche Hintergrund der prophetischen Gerichtsreden* (BZAW 85), Berlin, 1963, pp. 9ff., 20ff. Cf. also H. B. Huffmon, 'The Covenant Lawsuit in the Prophets', *JBL* 78, 1959, pp. 285ff. F. Hesse, 'Wurzelt die prophetische Gerichtsrede im israelitischen Kult?', *ZAW* 65, 1953, argues against Würthwein's suggestion by contending that before the time of Amos the cultic proclamation of Yahweh's judgment upon offenders was directed against foreign nations.

[2] Cf. C. Westermann, *Grundformen prophetischer Rede*, pp. 66ff., 70ff., 96.

they did. They understood the events of their times, and the advent of judgment, as directly related to Israel's flagrant violation of the covenant law. For them covenant, law and judgment were inseparably related factors which governed Yahweh's actions in the history of their days. The prophets must consequently be regarded, not simply as teachers of morality, but as the spokesmen of the covenant, for the morality which they taught implied the existence of a unique bond between Yahweh and Israel. The ethical standard which they knew was a code of covenant ethics, and even when they turned their attention to foreign nations, they judged them by the standard of conduct which they had learnt to expect of Israel.

The covenant cult proclaimed a basis of law which expressed Yahweh's demands and expectations of Israel, and the pre-exilic prophets interpreted and applied this law with a forcefulness which had not previously been heard. It is wrong, however, to regard the prophets simply as 'law-speakers', reiterating the neglected demands of a long-established covenant tradition. Even though the ideas, and even some of the speech-forms, used by the prophets originated in the covenant cult, we cannot accept the argument that an identity, or similarity, between the forms of speech used by two people necessarily implies that those speakers held an identical office. Such a conclusion goes beyond the legitimate results of form-criticism. It by no means follows, therefore, that the forms of speech which the prophets used, were still rooted in the institutions and situations in which those forms at first arose.[1] The prophets felt free to adopt a variety of forms, some of them of quite profane origin, as convenient vehicles of communication.[2] It is not surprising, therefore, that they took up the language, imagery and even some of the forms, that had grown up in the cult, where the covenant tradition was preserved, and reasserted the binding nature of its laws. They did this without necessarily intending to identify themselves with a particular

[1] Cf. G. Fohrer, 'Remarks on Modern Interpretation of the Prophets', *JBL* 80, 1961, pp. 311f.
[2] E.g., Isaiah utilizes the forms of the lawsuit (1.1–20), the love-song (5.1–7), and Wisdom teaching 28.23–29). Cf. S. Mowinckel, 'Literature', *IDB* III, p. 143a, 'During the ages the prophets have used the styles and forms of practically all the given poetic types, to make their sayings the more impressive.'

office of the covenant. This is the more readily intelligible when we recognize the direct concern of the prophetic message with the covenant, and the threat to its continued existence, which Israel's conduct presented. The prophets saw around them indifference to the law, and abuse of its institutions, which the cult of their day did nothing to rectify. The law was certainly not being effectively made known through the normal institutions and officials of the covenant. A grievous breakdown in the continuity of the Israelite tradition had occurred, which required the most forthright measures if Yahweh's will were really to be made known. The prophets, therefore, felt themselves charged with a kind of *officium extra ordinem*. They had no institutional position within the covenant, save that of prophecy in general, by which to authorize their message, but they needed none, since they knew that Yahweh had called them to deliver his word. We have seen the firmness with which Amos insisted upon the divine authority of his call to preach at Bethel. Yet this freedom from any institutional office did not mean that they were in any way indifferent to the covenant and its traditions. On the contrary, they actualized the demands of the covenant, in contrast to the corrupt and ineffective witness of the cult. The prophets insisted that their words served the true interests of the covenant, because they declared the true will of Yahweh, and the real nature of his actions towards Israel. The cult, on the contrary, only obscured Israel's understanding of Yahweh, by neglecting the demands of his law. Further we must argue for the distinctiveness of the prophetic vocation, as it was represented in. the canonical prophets, from the office of the covenant 'law-speaker', on the grounds of the radical interpretation of the law, which the prophets made. We have pointed out above that the curse of the law took on a new meaning in the prophets' threats of judgment upon Israel. Whilst we do not accept the claim of von Rad, that it was in the eighth-century prophets that for the first time the law took on a threatening aspect,[1] we must certainly accept that they interpreted the curse of the law in a new and radical way. Such a curse had always been a possibility, but now it threatened Israel in its entirety. In such stern preaching of the covenant law on the part of the prophets, we encounter a new moral earnestness, and a new primacy attached to the demand

[1] G. von Rad, *Old Testament Theology* I, p. 196.

for obedience. The demands of the law were stressed in a remarkable way, and its threatening aspect was used to interpret the turbulent history of the eighth, seventh and sixth centuries, in which Israel and Judah suffered so terribly. We cannot fit this radical interpretation of the curse of the law into the compass of the covenant festival cult, since it represents a very distinctive use of the ancient tradition of the law. It belongs so especially to the message of the great prophets of doom, and not to the earlier teaching of the cult, even though that cult certainly proclaimed both the laws demands, and its curse upon those who were disobedient to it. In their preaching of the law the pre-exilic prophets show the same tension between continuity and discontinuity with the past, which we have noted in other aspects of their activity and message. In many respects they continued a tradition of prophetic activity and preaching which already had a long history behind it, and yet they also broke with this tradition by their thoroughgoing insistence upon the primacy of obedience, and the appalling consequences of Israel's sin. There could be no patching-up of the covenant, nor any quick recovery from the wounds which Israel had inflicted upon itself. In their attitude to the law, therefore, we find a mixture of new and old, on the part of the pre-exilic prophets, which neither denies them their uniqueness and originality, nor ignores the long tradition of ethical religion which preceded them. The understanding of both the prophets and the law is illuminated by the recognition that they were both very much concerned with the covenant as the ground of Israel's life.[1]

In one other aspect of the form of their oracles it is clear that the use of the law in the cult has influenced the prophets. This is in the 'entrance liturgies', by which the cult sought to regulate access to the sanctuaries, and to prevent unsuitable persons from presenting themselves before Yahweh. The cultic prototype of such liturgies is well exemplified in Pss. 15 and 24.3–6.[2] These psalms

[1] E. Würthwein, 'Der Sinn des Gesetzes im Alten Testament', *ZTK* 55, 1958, p. 268.
[2] On these entrance-liturgies see S. Mowinckel, *Psalmenstudien* V, pp. 57ff., 107ff.; *The Psalms in Israel's Worship* I, pp. 177ff.; *Le décalogue*, pp. 141ff.; K. Galling, 'Der Beichtspiegel. Eine gattungsgeschichtliche Studie', *ZAW* 47, 1929, pp. 125ff.; K. Koch, 'Tempeleinlassliturgien und Dekaloge', *Studien zur Theologie der alttestamentlichen Überlieferungen*, ed. R. Rendtorff and K. Koch, Neukirchen, 1961, pp. 45ff.; J. L. Koole, *Psalm 15—eine königliche Einzugsliturgie?* (OTS 13), Leiden, 1963, pp. 98ff.

show a considerable development and elaboration from what must have been the rather primitive kinds of taboos which precluded some would-be worshippers from entering the sanctuaries at an earlier time, and in other religious environments. These particular examples of Israelite entrance-liturgies are of a profoundly ethical character, and the use of such terms of entry, if taken seriously, by inculcating a right understanding of Yahweh's demands would have contributed towards raising the moral standards of society. The declaration of the divine will in this fashion presented a challenge to everyone who sought to approach Yahweh in the cult.[1] S. Mowinckel at one time argued that the present Ethical Decalogue of Ex. 20.2–17 was developed out of the form of these entrance-liturgies.[2] In his more recent work, however, Mowinckel concedes that the main cultic ceremonies of Israel contained a declaration of the law, which cannot be divorced from the decalogic form, so that we have two parallel cultic phenomena and developments of Israel's ritual.[3] It seems in fact very probable that it was the strongly ethical note of the Decalogue, proclaimed as a central feature of the covenant cult, which led to the transforming of the entrance *tōrōth* from a series of taboos into a declaration of the ethical demands of Yahweh.

This particular use of the law, which took place in the cult, provided a form of presentation of the demands of Yahweh, which the prophets could emulate. Such prophetic imitations of the entrance-liturgies of Israel's sanctuaries are to be found in Isa. 33.14–16 and Micah 6.6–8. The former of these in particular shows a very close adherence to the original cultic form:

> Hear, you who are far off, what I have done;
>> and you who are near, acknowledge my might.
> The sinners in Zion are afraid;
>> trembling has seized the godless;

[1] J. L. Koole, *op. cit.*, pp. 98ff., argues that Psalm 15 is not an entrance-liturgy for all Israelites, but was used in the rites of the accession of the king to the throne. He maintains that entrance to the sanctuary was controlled by cultic stipulations only, and that sinners can hardly have been debarred from the means of forgiveness. These objections disappear, however, when we recognize the admonitory nature of these requirements, which affected every Israelite in his daily life, and which are less directly relevant for a king. See also my article 'Temple and Land. A Significant Aspect of Israel's Worship' (*TGUOS* 19) for the relevance of such liturgies to daily life.

[2] S. Mowinckel, *Le décalogue*, pp. 141ff.

[3] S. Mowinckel, *The Psalms in Israel's Worship* I, p. 180 note.

'Who among us can dwell with the devouring fire?
  Who among us can dwell with the perpetual burnings?'
He who walks righteously and speaks uprightly;
  he who despises the gain of oppressions,
who shakes his hands, lest they hold a bribe,
  who stops his ears from hearing of bloodshed,
  and shuts his eyes from looking upon evil.
He will dwell on the heights;
  his place of defence will be the fortresses of rocks;
  his bread will be given him, his water will be sure.
                    (Isa. 33.13–16.)[1]

The example in Micah 6.6–8 shows a greater freedom on the part of the prophet, especially as regards the content of the oracle. The cultic form is used to present some of the most insistent demands of the prophetic message. We must beware, therefore, of making too precise an identification of the form of an oracle with its content. Although naturally the prophets adopted various forms, with which to clothe their message, it is a misconception to make a total identification of form with content. Clearly these two examples are not actual entrance-liturgies of the cult, but oracles modelled on them. It would be even more erroneous to suppose that because the prophets used this form, they were themselves fulfilling the office of the sanctuary doorkeepers. Nevertheless there is a similarity between the task which confronted the prophet, and that which ought to have concerned every priest. This task was that of making known the real nature of Yahweh, and how men could find fellowship with him. For both, the basis of their faith was to be found in the covenant, with its claim upon Israel to be obedient to its laws.

In view of the general neglect of Yahweh's law, and the widespread disregard of its injunctions, which the prophets found, we must remain very sceptical about the actual influence upon Israel of such a cultic torah-liturgy during the period of the monarchy.[2]

[1] H. Gunkel, 'Jesaia 33, eine prophetische Liturgie', *ZAW* 42, 1924, pp. 177ff., endeavoured to trace in Isaiah 33 a 'prophetic liturgy' of which the entrance liturgy of verses 14b–16 formed a part.

[2] It is very probable that there were priests in Jerusalem who were genuinely concerned to make known the will of Yahweh through the medium of such entrance-liturgies, as K. Koch argues, 'Tempeleinlassliturgien und Dekaloge', *Studien zur Theologie*, ed. Rendtorff and Koch, p. 59. This does not mean that they were necessarily all that effective in doing so,

The examples which we have in the Psalter are distinctly Jerusalem-Judean developments, and in the sanctuaries of the Northern Kingdom it is possible that such a presentation of the ethical demands of worship found little or no place. Their use in the Jerusalem temple also may easily have become so formal and accepted that it provoked little challenge to many worshippers.

Behind the prophets we must certainly recognize the existence of a well-developed tradition of law, which embraced the whole round of Israelite life. This strongly ethical claim of religion was rooted in the covenant, and its injunctions sought to prevent any conduct detrimental to the life and welfare of the covenant people. Yet the prophets found this law held in little regard, and openly flouted in innumerable ways, so that they stressed as never before the threatening aspect which that law contained. Israel had placed itself under the judgment of the law, and had been found guilty. Instead of the law being the source of the nation's welfare and happiness, it had become a curse and a threat to its continued existence. The open disregard of the law in the society which the pre-exilic prophets knew, is evidence of a general breakdown in the preservation and enforcement of the covenant tradition. Israel did not do the will of Yahweh, because no longer was it effectively being made known, and the responsibility for this ignorance was primarily to be laid upon the ministers and institutions of the cult.

---

especially in the face of the power of the wealthy landowners and governing class. Such response as these priestly efforts provoked did not measure up to the rigorous demands of Isaiah and Jeremiah for a true righteousness and loyalty to Yahweh.

V

ISRAEL'S WORSHIP AND THE PRE-EXILIC PROPHETS

OUR examination, in the preceding chapter, of the attitude of the pre-exilic prophets to Israel's law has illuminated the fact that the natural home of this law was in the cult. The failure of the law to prevent a dissolution of moral standards in Israelite society was fundamentally a failure of the cult to make known a true knowledge of Yahweh. The law failed to be an effective force in governing Israelite behaviour, because the cult failed to make known the true demands of the covenant. As a consequence the forceful affirmations of the injunctions of the covenant law by the prophets stand in marked contrast to the neglect of the covenant demands in the worship of Israel's sanctuaries. Yet this neglect of the covenant law in the Israelite cult was not paralleled by any neglect of the cult itself, nor by any disregard of its rites. On the contrary, the evidence of the prophetic books shows that everywhere throughout the land the sanctuaries flourished, their priests were held in high regard and the festivals were eagerly attended by great masses of the people. The cult had become a very potent force in Israelite life, without, in the estimation of the prophets, representing the true will of Yahweh. It is therefore a natural sequel to our study of the attitude of the prophets to Israel's law that we should examine what they had to say about Israel's worship.

We may preface such a study by a few brief words regarding the cultic nature of Israelite religion.[1] From the earliest period of which we have any clear picture of Israel's religion, it is certain that that religion was cultic in its expression. There was no purely individualistic piety which divorced itself from the public ceremonies and festivals which governed the devotion of the people as

[1] For a brief study of the nature and meaning of cult see S. Mowinckel, *Religion und Kultus*, pp. 10ff., 60ff.

a whole. To have abandoned the Israelite cult would have been tantamount to abandoning allegiance to Yahweh.[1] We have seen that the very foundation of Israelite life was its covenant relationship to Yahweh, which was affirmed through certain cultic rites. The covenant festival was the centre of the entire people's religious devotion. This does not deny that more individual prayers and acts of piety were practised by Israelites, but such were not regarded as substitutes for the normal round of public worship. Further, we must recognize that such cult was not simply a performance of outward ceremonies which did not touch the heart of every Israelite. We have already pointed out that it was a very important responsibility of the sanctuaries and their priests to inculcate in each worshipper a right attitude to Yahweh, and a right knowledge of him. By the spoken word, by visual symbolism, as well as by the accomplished act, the worship of the shrines was designed to communicate a knowledge of true religion. The sanctuaries and festivals were not only means whereby men found access to God, but they were also the organs for communicating a right knowledge of God to men. The personal piety of each Israelite was very much moulded by the attitudes and traditions fostered by the corporate worship of the sanctuaries. In fact it is misleading to make a sharp contrast in early Israel between corporate and personal piety, since the public worship guided and stimulated individual devotion, and certainly it would be wrong to suppose that the cult was only interested in performing certain ceremonies without regarding the individual's response to them.[2] The cult had a teaching function which must not be neglected or relegated to a position of small importance. In a world where literacy was attained only by a few, and where the use of literature was restricted, the cult had the primary place as a means of religious instruction. The sacred shrine was the most powerful agency of continuity in religion, and the hereditary priesthood, which normally attended it, passed on from one generation to another

[1] This is the underlying reasoning behind David's answer to Saul in I Sam. 26.19. To be alienated from the sanctuaries of Yahweh meant being alienated from worshipping him.

[2] Cf. H. Ringgren, *The Faith of the Psalmists*, London, 1963, pp. 20ff., for the relationship between personal piety and the cult, and also G. E. Mendenhall, 'The Relation of the Individual to Political Society in Ancient Israel', *Biblical Studies in Memory of H. C. Alleman, passim.*

the holy lore that had been entrusted to them.[1] 'Like people, like priest' (Hos. 4.9) was a fundamental fact of religion, since the priests held the key to the knowledge of God, and few others could lay claim to an equal possession of such knowledge. The more tenuous traditions of individual families and tribes were less reliable sources for an understanding of Yahweh. With the adoption by Israel of a settled way of life, and of an urban social order, the tribal continuity was largely broken, and only when jealously guarded, as in the case of the Rechabites, did it offer a well-preserved tradition of Yahweh worship. The sanctuaries and priests were the accepted guardians of religious truth, and all who desired to know the nature and will of Yahweh brought their enquiries to the sanctuary. We have already seen that it was normal for the prophets to officiate at the sanctuaries, especially during the festivals, so that they, like their priestly colleagues, could declare the divine instruction (Heb. *tōrāh*).[2] It is a false understanding of ancient religion to suppose that its cult was solely concerned with the repetition of traditional rites, which were regarded as automatically effective, or that a developed cult was solely the prerogative of a religious concern with the blessing and fertility of the natural order. Cult was fundamental to all ancient religion, since it was through it that religion found its corporate expression, and a communication of religious ideas took place.

The substance of Israel's cult was certainly not of a single unified origin, any more than the Israelites themselves were derived from a single family stock. Every increase in our knowledge of the Canaanite cult has served to show how deeply the Israelites were indebted to the Canaanites for the forms of their worship.[3]

[1] On the importance of the cult in maintaining the continuity of Israelite religion see P. R. Ackroyd, *Continuity. A Contribution to the Study of the Old Testament Religious Tradition*, Oxford, 1962, pp. 20ff.; R. Gyllenberg, 'Kultus und Offenbarung', *Interpretationes ad Vetus Testamentum pertinentes Sigmundo Mowinckel*, Oslo, 1955, pp. 72ff. Cf. also B. S. Childs, *Memory and Tradition in Israel* (SBT 37), London, 1962, pp. 53ff.

[2] For the meaning of *torah*, and its different sources and exponents see G. Östborn, *Tora in the Old Testament. A Semantic Study*, Lund, 1945. The claim of J. Begrich, *Die priesterliche Tora* (BZAW 66), Berlin, 1938, pp. 63ff., that the priestly torah was dominated by the concepts of 'clean' and 'unclean', 'holy' and 'profane', cannot be maintained.

[3] Cf. J. Pedersen, 'Canaanite and Israelite Cultus', *AO* 18, 1940, pp. 1ff.; J. Gray, 'Cultic Affinities between Israel and Ras Shamra', *ZAW* 62, 1949-50, pp. 207ff.

The types of sacrifice, the festival calendar and often the very sanctuaries themselves were taken over from the Canaanites.[1] The latter fact was naturally a material cause of the first two. When Israel settled in Canaan, and eventually under David gained complete control of the land, the old shrines were adopted and used for the worship of Yahweh. Much of the older pattern of cult was continued, but was transformed because it was now in honour of Yahweh.[2] So heavy is this borrowing from Canaan that it is now beyond the powers of the historian to make any probable reconstruction of what Israel's cult was like when the people first settled in the land. In the days of the amphictyony we know that the tradition of the covenant formed the centre of Israel's religious life, but alongside this a wide variety of local cultic traditions must have continued in existence. Before their conversion to Yahwism, many of the sanctuaries which Israel used had been the centres of El and Baal worship, whilst some proto-Israelite groups must have continued to reverence the gods of the patriarchs. In the days before the monarchy no uniformity existed because there was no agency which could enforce it.[3] Only a general ethos served to provide some measure of conformity. The exclusive claims of Israel's own covenant tradition extended just as far as membership of that covenant was felt to extend. The task of defining the character of the cult practised at the different sanctuaries is fraught with uncertainties for the historian. Shechem has justifiably been regarded as a vital centre for the maintenance of the Yahwistic covenant tradition on account of the record of a great covenant assembly there under the leadership of Joshua (Josh. 24.1ff.).[4]

[1] For the Canaanite origin of Israel's sacrificial system see R. Dussaud, *Les origines Cananéennes du sacrifice Israelite* (rev. ed.), Paris, 1941. However, whilst much of the sacrificial system of Israel was taken over from Canaan, it is very improbable that in the Mosaic period Israel's religion was wholly without sacrifice. Cf. H. H. Rowley, 'The Meaning of Sacrifice in the Old Testament', *From Moses to Qumran*, London, 1963, pp. 72ff.

[2] Cf. A. C. Welch, *Prophet and Priest in Old Israel*, rep. Oxford, 1953, p. 58, 'There was no great difference in the rituals which Israel practised, except that these were performed in honour of its own God.'

[3] Joshua's address at the Assembly of Shechem (Josh. 24.1ff.), presupposes that early Israel was faced with a real choice between Yahwism, the worship of the patriarchal gods, and the worship of the Canaanite gods (v. 15). Cf. G. E. Mendenhall, 'Election', *IDB* II, p. 77b.

[4] M. Noth, *Das System der Zwölf Stämme Israels*, pp. 65ff.; *Das Buch Josua* (HAT), 2 Aufl., 1953, pp. 135ff. Cf. also H. J. Kraus, *Gottesdienst in Israel*

The account of the proceedings stresses very forcibly the necessity of loyalty to Yahweh, and the repudiation of alien deities. We cannot doubt that Shechem was at one time the cult-centre of the Israelite amphictyony, and yet even here the Old Testament gives evidence of the cult of a Canaanite god, El-Berith, or Baal-Berith (Judg. 8.33; 9.4, 46), which must have continued in close proximity to the Israelite worship of Yahweh. The very fact that the name of the Canaanite god was God (or Lord) of the covenant, tempts us into considering some kind of connexion with the Israelite shrine there.[1]

Gilgal also became a cult-centre of great importance for Israel's covenant tradition, and seems to have been especially related to a recollection of the conquest, and of Yahweh's gift of the land of Canaan to Israel.[2] The circle of stones there (Josh. 4.1–9, 20–22), which must have been in existence from a very much earlier period than that of the Israelite conquest, signifies the ancient cultic associations of the place which gave it its name (Heb. *gilgal* = circle [of stones]). At one time the sanctuary of Gilgal possessed the ark, as the narratives of the Book of Joshua relate, so that it

(2 Aufl.), 1962, pp. 161ff. A study of the place of Shechem in the development of the Israelite religious tradition is made by E. Nielsen, *Shechem: A Traditio-historical Investigation*, Copenhagen, 1955. A more positive approach is made in 'Shechem, Navel of the Land', *BA* 20, 1957 pp. 2ff., by W. Harrelson, B. W. Anderson and G. E. Wright. I have not seen the unpublished thesis of W. Harrelson, *The City of Shechem, its History and Interpretation*, Union Theological Seminary, New York, 1953.

[1] This covenant is probably connected with the name Hamor (= ass) mentioned in Gen. 33.19 and Judg. 9.28 as that of the father of Shechem. Such a name reflects the custom of slaughtering an ass to make a covenant (cf. Jer. 34.18–19). See W. F. Albright, *From the Stone Age to Christianity* (2nd ed.), 1957, p. 279, and F. Willesen, 'Die Eselsöhne von Sichem als Bundesgenossen', *VT* 4, 1954, pp. 216f. C. Steuernagel, 'Jahwe der Gott Israels. Eine stil- und religionsgeschichtliche Studie', *J. Wellhausen Festschrift* (BZAW 27), Giessen, 1914, pp. 329ff., argued that the title, 'Yahweh, the God of Israel' was once bound to the cult-site of Shechem. More recently R. Smend, *Die Bundesformel*, pp. 14f., has stressed the connexion of the name Israel with Shechem, and has argued that in pre-Yahwistic times there was worshipped there a Canaanite deity, El-elohe-Israel (cf. Gen. 33.20). V. Maag, 'Der Hirte Israels', *Schweizerische theologische Umschau* 28, 1958, pp. 8f., on the other hand, has sought to trace here a patriarchal god, similar to the other such deities, known as 'the Shepherd of Israel' (cf. Gen. 49.24).

[2] Cf. H. J. Kraus, 'Gilgal', *VT* 1, 1951, pp. 181ff.; and *Gottesdienst in Israel* (2 Aufl.), pp. 179ff.; H. Wildberger, *Jahwes Eigentumsvolk*, pp. 55ff., seeks to locate Israel's particular 'election tradition', which he separates from that of the covenant, at Gilgal, and connects this with the pericope of Ex. 19.3b–8.

may have served as a centre for the Israelite amphictyony. Bethel also was an ancient sanctuary of very great influence, which was claimed by the Israelites as a foundation of the patriarch Jacob (Gen. 28.10–22).[1] The fact that Jereboam I took steps to make Bethel a leading centre of Israel's religion after the disruption of the Davidic empire at Solomon's death (I Kings 12.29, 32f.), and to introduce the tradition of the exodus there, suggests that before this time it may have had only a very loose relationship to the Israelite covenant.[2]

The far-reaching changes in Israel's social and religious order, which were introduced by David with the formation of the Israelite State, led to a very positive claim to define Israel's nationhood by its territorial boundaries. Thus many diverse elements of population, and a great variety of sanctuaries, were incorporated into the new State of Israel, and although they were nominally unified under the king as the one religious and political head, it was many centuries before a strong national and religious consciousness came to pervade all those who now called themselves Israelites. Under David the old amphictyonic cult-centre was transferred permanently to Jerusalem, and the ark was installed there. Yet even in Jerusalem, with its sacred Mount Zion where Solomon built a temple, we know that many notable innovations of a religious nature were introduced into Israel. These were largely a consequence of the adoption by Israel of much of the earlier Jebusite cult of El-ʿElyon.[3] It was natural that the Jerusalem temple, with its royal support and its claim to represent the authentic covenant tradition of Israel, should have boasted precedence over other shrines. Yet this was far from being conceded,

[1] At one time the sanctuary of Bethel had some relationship to the worship of the deity Bethel, who continued for a long period to be revered in Canaanite, and the less-orthodox Israelite, circles. See especially O. Eissfeldt, 'Der Gott Bethel', *Kleine Schriften* I, Tübingen, 1962, pp. 206ff., who finds evidence of such a god in the Old Testament in Jer. 48.13; Amos 3.14b; 5.4, 6; Hos. 10.15; 12.5 (EVV 4). See also J. P. Hyatt, 'The Deity Bethel and the Old Testament', *JAOS* 59, 1939, pp. 81–98.

[2] Israel is associated with Bethel in Judg. 20.26–27; cf. Judg. 20.18; 21.2. M. Noth, *The History of Israel*, p. 94, suggests that at one time the ark was at Bethel, but this is uncertain, and it is very plausible that the connexion of early Israel with Bethel may well be an anachronism introduced into Israelite traditions after the time of Jeroboam I. Cf. M. L. Newman, *The People of the Covenant*, p. 60.

[3] See above pp. 59f.

and was openly repudiated by Northern Israel after the death of Solomon. Where the primacy of Jerusalem was accepted there was still no guarantee of orthodoxy, since the Jerusalem tradition itself, with its attachment to the royal court, had introduced extensive modifications and additions to the earlier covenant tradition. In particular the building of a temple had meant a great increase and elaboration of the rites and ceremonies associated with the worship of Yahweh. The old covenant tradition was very much forced into the background by the pretentiousness of the new order.[1]

There is little to dispel our impression that during the period of the monarchy there was as much variety and multiformity of worship at the different sanctuaries of Israel, as there had been in the days before. No single shrine was accorded absolute precedence over all the others, although Jerusalem was obviously the most significant of Israel's sanctuaries. In the Northern Kingdom the importance of Jerusalem was openly and vigorously disavowed (I Kings 12.26ff.). In Jerusalem a considerable change was brought about by the reform of Josiah (621 BC), when a genuine effort was made to reinterpret the meaning and significance of Jerusalem and its worship in accordance with the ancient tradition of the covenant on Mount Sinai. At the same time the remaining sanctuaries outside Jerusalem, which had not fallen to Assyrian power, were suppressed. All this took place, however, only after the protests of the great prophets of the eighth century had been made. The same is true of any reforms which Hezekieh may have introduced (II Kings 18.3ff.).

It is apparent that whilst Israel's cult was the primary means of preserving some continuity of faith and allegiance to Yahweh, that cult could only give a very uncertain witness. The power of the throne was the only force which could support, or suppress, the claims of individual sanctuaries, since no natural, or historical, precedence was conceded. It is understandable therefore that

[1] I cannot therefore agree entirely with A. Weiser, *The Psalms*, p. 26, when he claims that the Jerusalem temple, with its festivals, represented the genuinely Israelite tradition of Yahweh during the period of the monarchy. Whilst there was much of the covenant tradition preserved at Jerusalem there was also much else besides. The reform of Josiah was of great importance in pruning away from the Jerusalem cultus the more unacceptable accretions to the Israelite tradition.

sanctuaries such as Jerusalem, Bethel and Dan, which enjoyed royal support, were thereby helped to raise themselves above the others. Yet this royal support was not governed by any genuine discernment into the meaning of the Israelite tradition, or by a desire to preserve what was most authentic in the nation's faith. Rather it was very much at the whim of the monarch, or the necessities of political intrigue.[1] If the cult was responsible for expressing the authentic word of Yahweh, that word had become very much obscured by the diversity of cultic traditions and practice.

We find during the pre-exilic period, therefore, that Israel's cult was of immense importance as an instrument for maintaining a continuity of faith and conduct in Israel, whilst in actual fact no clear pattern of uniformity served to guide and to control that cult. The earlier Mosaic traditions of Yahwism were preserved alongside, and intermingled with, the more elaborate cultic institutions and practices which had been borrowed from the Canaanites. We must accept the fact that there were considerable regional differences between the rites and traditions preserved in different parts of Israel's territory, and that the sanctuaries and their priests each guarded their own particular tradition very tenaciously. No one sanctuary, nor any one priesthood, maintained the simplicity of the original covenant tradition, although each of them no doubt claimed to do so. In part such a situation was the inevitable consequence of the piecemeal adoption of many features of Canaanite cult, without any selective evaluation of its worth, or of its compatability with Israel's covenant faith. In the outcome it is apparent that the Mosaic covenant tradition had been largely fragmented through the diversity and rival claims of the many shrines which flourished in the two kingdoms of Israel and Judah.[2]

It is only by bearing in mind this background of the crisis which came into Israel's cultic life during the period of the monarchy, that we can understand the attitude of the prophets to Israel's cult. The failure of the cult to uphold the demands of

[1] Cf. the prophetic and priestly support for Solomon's accession to the throne, with the banishment of the house of Abiathar from the Jerusalem priesthood (I Kings 2.26f.). Undoubtedly Abiathar's claim to the priesthood of Israel's chief shrine had a stronger justification on the grounds of inheritance and tradition than did Zadok's.

[2] Cf. N. W. Porteous, 'The Prophets and the Problem of Continuity', *Israel's Prophetic Heritage*, ed. Anderson and Harrelson, pp. 17ff.; G. Fohrer, 'Remarks on Modern Interpretation of the Prophets', *JBL* 80, 1961, p. 314.

Israel's law was only one part of its wider failure to represent the interests of the covenant as a whole. The great prophets of the eighth and seventh centuries intervened in this situation to re-awaken a knowledge of what the covenant really meant, and in doing so they strenuously attacked the contemporary worship of the sanctuaries:

> For thus says Yahweh to the house of Israel:
>   'Seek me and live;
>   but do not seek Bethel,
>   and do not enter into Gilgal
>   or cross over to Beer-sheba;
>   for Gilgal shall surely go into exile,
>   and Bethel shall come to naught.'
>   (Amos 5.4–5.)

Amos insisted that the festivals, with their sacrifices, in no way served the will of Yahweh:

> I hate, I despise your feasts,
>   and I take no delight in your solemn assemblies.
> Even though you offer me your burnt offerings and cereal offerings,
>   I will not accept them,
> and the communion offerings of your fattened beasts
>   I will not look upon.
> Take away from me the noise of your songs;
>   to the melody of your harps I will not listen.
> But let justice roll down like waters,
>   and righteousness like an everflowing stream.
>   (Amos 5.21–24.)

In conclusion the prophet declared that the offering of sacrifices represented no part of the original covenant tradition:

> Did your bring me sacrifices and offerings the forty years in the wilderness, O house of Israel?'
>   (Amos 5.25.)

Hosea also opposed the offering of sacrifices when they were divorced from the true knowledge of Yahweh:

> For I desire true loyalty and not sacrifice,
>   the knowledge of God, rather than burnt offerings.
>   (Hos. 6.6; cf. also Jer. 7.21–23; Isa. 1.11–17; Micah 6.6–8.)

This radical rejection of the contemporary cult by the pre-exilic prophets has figured prominently in modern studies of Israel's religion. Some scholars have claimed that these pre-exilic prophets were giving expression to a total rejection of all cult in the interests of a more spiritual religion.[1] This view has necessarily undergone considerable criticism and some modification in the light of a closer examination of the evidence contained in the Old Testament.[2] In its radical form we must abandon it, since it is clear that what these prophets rejected was not the cult as such, for its own sake, but the cult which had become divorced from righteousness and obedience to Yahweh. The very fact that the prophetic criticisms stress righteousness and justice over against the offering of sacrifices, points to the relative, rather than absolute, nature of their opposition to the worship of the sanctuaries. They did not oppose all cult as such, in favour of a non-cultic religion, but they opposed the cult which they found because it no longer expressed the ethical nature of true Yahwism. We have already pointed out that some measure of historical justification did exist for the claim that Israel's sacrificial practice did not originate in the wilderness, with the formation of the covenant, but stemmed from subsequent

---

[1] So P. Volz, 'Die radikale Ablehnung der Kultreligion durch die alttestamentlichen Propheten', *Zeitschrift für systematische Theologie* 14, 1937, pp. 63ff.; R. Hentschke, *Die Stellung der vorexilischen Schriftpropheten zum Kultus*, pp. 74ff., 88ff., and C. F. Whitley, *The Prophetic Achievement*, pp. 63ff.

[2] See especially H. H. Rowley, *The Rediscovery of the Old Testament*, London, 1945, pp. 109ff., 117ff., 122; *The Unity of the Bible*, London, 1953, pp. 30ff., 127; *The Faith of Israel*, London, 1956, pp. 136ff., and 'The Meaning of Sacrifice in the Old Testament', *From Moses to Qumran, passim*. Cf. also Rowley's exchange with C. J. Cadoux: 'The Religious Value of Sacrifice', *ExpT* 58, 1946–7, pp. 69–71, against Cadoux's 'The Religious Value of Sacrifice', *ibid.*, pp. 43–46, and with N. H. Snaith: 'The Prophets and Sacrifice', *ExpT* 58, 1946–7, pp. 305–7, against Snaith's 'The Prophets and Sacrifice', *ibid.*, pp. 152–3. See also K. Roubos, *Profetie en Cultus in Israël*, Wageningen, 1956, who stresses that the prophets did not condemn the cult as such, but the attitude of Israelites to it. H. Ringgren, *Sacrifice in the Bible* (World Christian Books 42), London, 1962, pp. 54ff.; J. Lindblom, *Prophecy in Ancient Israel*, pp. 351ff.; E. Sjöberg, 'De förexiliska profeternas förkunnelse. Några synpunkter', *SEA* 14, 1949, pp. 13ff. A new insight into the criticism of the cult by the prophets is suggested by R. Rendtorff, 'Priesterliche Kulttheologie und prophetische Kultpolemik', *TLZ* 81, 1956, cols. 339ff., who draws attention to the distinctive cultic terminology used by the prophets in their polemic. This examination is carried still further by E. Würthwein, 'Kultpolemik oder Kultbescheid?', *Tradition und Situation*, pp. 115ff., who argues that the prophetic criticisms betray a dependence on a common tradition, both in form and language. This tradition, he suggests, originated in the divine response, given in the cult, to rites of penitence and fasting, which the prophets have imitated in a negative fashion.

Canaanite influence. Exactly what kind of cult did exist in the wilderness we do not know. It is very improbable that it was wholly non-sacrificial, but it was sufficient for Amos and Jeremiah to know that the cult which they found practised in Israel did not represent the covenant tradition. A religion without moral obedience, however elaborate its ceremonies and festivals, did not fulfil the demands of the holy God of Israel. The great canonical prophets of the period before the exile rejected the contemporary cult on the grounds that it did not represent the authentic tradition of the covenant. This is clearly hinted at by Hosea in contrasting the 'knowledge of God' with the giving of burnt offerings (Hos. 6.6). This 'knowledge of God', as we have seen, signified a knowledge of the covenant tradition, with its declaration of the origin of the covenant in Yahweh's acts of grace and the law which presented his demands upon his people. The practice of true loyalty and righteousness should have been the fruits of Israel's knowledge of its God.[1] When the sacrificial worship of Israel had obscured and replaced this knowledge of Yahweh's covenant, it had ceased to honour Yahweh, and had failed to fulfil its essential task of making known his will. We must couple the prophetic attack upon sacrifices, therefore, with the insistence by the prophets that the authentic knowledge of Yahweh had ceased out of the land. Both alike represent a criticism of the cult, and an allegation that it had become unfaithful to the covenant which it was intended to serve, and which was fundamental to Israel's life:

> My people are destroyed for lack of knowledge;
>> because you have rejected knowledge,
>> I reject you from being a priest to me.
> And since you have forgotten the law of your God,
>> I also will forget your children.
>
> (Hos. 4.6; cf. 5.1.)
>
> Therefore my people go into exile for want of knowledge;
>> their honoured men are dying of hunger,
>> and their multitude is parched with thirst.
>
> (Isa. 5.13.)

The people of Israel walked in ignorance of Yahweh because the accepted means of communicating a knowledge of him, the cult, had entirely failed in its purpose. Instead it had become over-

[1] Cf. H. W. Wolff, ' "Wissen um Gott" bei Hosea als Urform von Theologie', *EvTh* 12, 1952–3, pp. 547f.

loaded with rites and ceremonies, borrowed from the Canaanites, which had never been integrated into the older Mosaic tradition. Old and new, good and bad, all lay side by side in a pattern of cultic observance which obscured whatever elements it retained of the authentic covenant tradition. This does not deny that such elements were present in the cult, but it is clear from the reproaches of the prophets, that they were not readily apparent to the majority of the people. Instead, the least agreeable aspects of Canaanite worship, its emphasis upon fertility, and the power of correctly performed rituals to achieve the divine blessing, tended to be emphasized and enforced. Israel's covenant tradition had been fragmented in the cult into a multitude of heterogeneous ceremonies, which had little relation to each other, or to the God who had first called Israel into being.

The recent emphasis in Old Testament research upon the creative aspects of the cult, and its importance for the continuity of Israel's faith, serves to illuminate the picture that we have of the tragic consequences of the break-up and failure of that cult. What the prophets encountered was not just the apostasy of this or that sanctuary, or priesthood, but a general confusion and diversity, which left little evidence of the authentic voice of Yahweh. Whilst from our knowledge of the Psalms, many of which are of an early pre-exilic date, it is apparent that the traditions of Israel's covenant, and of the nation's election at the exodus, were never wholly lost, yet in the mixed situation which the prophets found, such traditions were not given a rightful priority. The cult and the priesthood had failed in their obligation to teach the true knowledge of Yahweh, so that Amos, and the other prophets of judgment, found it necessary to attack the pattern of worship which they found. The point at issue was a dispute as to where the authentic word of Yahweh's covenant was to be heard. These prophets insisted that such a word was to be found in their prophecies, and not in the teaching of the priests and prophets at the shrines.

It is apparent from the evidence of the Old Testament itself that the canonical prophets were not the only ones to protest against the Canaanizing of Israel's life and worship. Such groups as the Rechabites made a very resolute protest against everything which they considered opposed to the older traditions of Israel. Also we find that Amos could point to the presence of prophets and Nazirites in Israel as evidence of the maintenance of a faithful witness to Yahweh (Amos 2.11–12). The very fact that all of the canonical prophets show themselves familiar with the historical traditions about Israel's origin betokens the presence of men who did keep alive such a knowledge of Yahweh. Often this had to be done in spite of, or even in opposition to, the sanctuaries. It is natural in this regard to think of the groups of Levites who had their settlements in parts of Israel, and who regarded themselves as especially entrusted with the religious traditions of their people. H. W. Wolff has ventured the suggestion that the activity of such levitical groups may lie behind the prophecies of Hosea.[1] If so, then the prophet's own religious experience was nurtured in the traditions which they cherished. It is in every way probable that the composition of the Deuteronomic edition of Israel's covenant law, with its long introductory discourses, is the product of many years of reflection and preaching activity on the part of Levites.[2] In this case we must see that the relationship of Deuteronomy and the Deuteronomic reformation to the eighth- and seventh-century prophets is not one of direct influence of the latter upon the former, but was less direct. Both the prophets and the Deuteronomic law-book were influenced by the levitical groups who guarded so carefully the ancient traditions of Israel.[3] This makes intelligible the fact that prophecy is only given a small place in Deuteronomy, and is subjected to critical regulations which would be hard to understand if Deuteronomy were itself so dependent upon the inspiration of the prophets. Besides such groups of Levites we must not overlook the importance of the guilds of prophets, who were not all attached to individual sanctuaries, and who kept alive their own distinctive heritage. The communication of a knowledge of Yahweh, therefore, whilst it was primarily in

[1] H. W. Wolff, 'Hoseas geistige Heimat', *TLZ* 81, 1956, cols. 91ff.; ' "Wissen um Gott" bei Hosea als Urform von Theologie', *EvTh* 12, p. 553.

[2] A. Bentzen, *Die josianische Reform und ihre Voraussetzungen*, Copenhagen, 1926, pp. 58ff.; G. von Rad, *Das Gottesvolk im Deuteronomium*, pp. 78ff.; *Studies in Deuteronomy* (SBT 9), London, 1953, p. 66; *Old Testament Theology* I, p. 221; 'Deuteronomy', *IDB* I, p. 836a. For the place of the Levites in Israel see K. Möhlenbrink, 'Die levitischen Überlieferungen des Alten Testaments', *ZAW* 52, 1934, pp. 184ff.; R. de Vaux, *Ancient Israel*, pp. 358ff.

[3] Cf. N. W. Porteous, 'Actualization and the Prophetic Criticism of the Cult', *Tradition und Situation*, ed. Würthwein and Kaiser, pp. 99f.

the hands of the sanctuaries and their priests, was not exclusively limited to them. Other groups, who sometimes lived in quite separate and self-contained communities, did endeavour to maintain a true knowledge of Yahweh, and of what his covenant demands upon Israel really meant.[1] This fact is important for an understanding of the problem of continuity in Israelite religion. Whilst it was generally to be expected that such a continuity would be provided by the sanctuaries and their cult, it was not exclusively so. In fact during the eighth and seventh centuries the cult failed very lamentably in this regard. The covenant tradition had become broken and obscured in the diversity of practice at Israel's sanctuaries. Various individual groups, who isolated themselves to some extent from the major cities and sanctuaries, sought to be faithful to the older Mosaic tradition. Then in the great prophets a more forthright and public challenge to the teaching and practice of the cult was made. Amos and Hosea claimed to speak the true word of Yahweh, and rejected the claims of the sanctuaries to serve Yahweh. They had become false and worthless, and a knowledge of God had ceased out of the land. These prophets, by rejecting the sacrificial worship of the shrines, did so on account of the failure of such cult to accord with the nature and demands of the covenant. The prophets, and not the cult of the sanctuaries, made known the true will of Yahweh.

The issue at stake in the eighth and seventh centuries was, 'Where is the true knowledge of Yahweh to be found?' Historically and institutionally this knowledge should have been found at the sanctuaries of Israel. Here the priests were the custodians of tradition, and the worship and festivals were the accepted means of reminding Israel of its obligations, and instructing the people into the way of Yahweh. Prophecy, as a ministry of the covenant, belonged in this context of cultic institutions. Yet Amos, under the pressure of his call, was authorized to declare that the cult was a lie, and its blessings were just fictions. Far from declaring the will of Yahweh, and effecting communion with him, it misrepresented him, and obscured the basis of his covenant relationship to Israel. Amos rejected any restraints which tied prophecy to the sanctuaries, and he stood in opposition to the priests and cult of Bethel.

[1] Cf. N. W. Porteous, 'The Prophets and the Problem of Continuity', *Israel's Prophetic Heritage*, ed. Anderson and Harrelson, pp. 24f.

He could not align himself to the worship of the sanctuaries because he had to declare what the relationship of Israel to Yahweh really meant, and what judgment was about to fall upon the people. He claimed to be the true spokesman of Yahweh, and of his covenant, and opposed the worship at the sanctuaries which had become false to its origin and purpose. Hosea, even more forcefully than Amos, insisted that judgment would befall the priests because they had abandoned the true knowledge of Yahweh. This concerned not simply their own personal ignorance of him to whom they claimed to minister, but the betrayal of their office, in that they were authorized to be the true teachers of the way of Yahweh, but had abandoned this responsibility. They were not only deluding themselves, but were misleading the nation, by the way in which they neglected their service. As in the experience of Amos, so also with Hosea, it was the prophet and not the priest who truly represented the interests of the covenant.

We must understand the prophetic criticism of the cult, therefore, not as signifying that the prophets themselves desired a new kind of non-cultic religion on Israel's part. If we may conjecture what kind of reforms they would have sought to introduce, they would not have included the abolition of all cult, but its transformation to become a vehicle of a more ethical and responsible attitude towards Yahweh. Only so could it become a means of true communion with him. The condemnation of the cult lay not in the fact of its existence, but in the fact that it had abandoned the covenant tradition of Israel's past.

We must seek a positive assessment of the influence of prophecy upon Israelite and Jewish worship, by recognizing that the cult had established very positive forms and traditions before the rise of Amos. The prophets were not the creators of the spiritual and moral aspects which elevated Jewish worship and psalmography in the post-exilic age. Such aspects already held a place in the earliest traditions of Israelite devotion. Yet, whilst they did not create this nobler feeling for the service of Yahweh, the prophets played a vital and indispensable part in its preservation and development. In the days of the decline of the two Israelite kingdoms, when the great prophets appeared, Israel's cult had become crude and overloaded with alien accretions. Its finer aspects were submerged in a morass of rites and revelries which had little to do with the real service of God. By condemning these outright, and by insisting as never before on the priority of moral obedience in the service of Yahweh, the prophets initiated a new phase in the development of worship. In consequence it necessitated eventually that the priesthood should reconsider and revise its own traditions, and prune away the unworthy elements of the cult. Most especially did this occur during the period of the exile, when the truth of the prophetic warnings was so effectively vindicated. The considerable literary activity of the exilic and early post-exilic ages, when survivors of the disaster collected and pieced together the ancient traditions of their national past, did not ignore the preaching of the prophets. The task of sifting the old traditions, and of forming a literature which could serve as a guide for the reconstruction of Israel in the future, was carried out mindful of the voices of the prophets. The Old Testament, in the literary form that we possess, is the creation of the post-exilic era, and we must bear in mind that all those scribes and scholars to whom we owe its compilation and preservation lived in the aftermath of the golden age of prophecy. The traditionists of the law, of psalmography, of wisdom, as well as of prophecy, were all to be found in quite closely related circles that flourished after the exile. How Jewish worship was developed and shaped for the future owes a great debt to the particular condemnations and emphases which the pre-exilic prophets had made. In this way, out of the fragments of a broken tradition of the Yahwistic cult, which was all that remained for Israel during the days of the monarchy, there gradually appeared a clear and firm insistence upon the moral and spiritual nature of the service of Yahweh. The preaching of the prophets was an indispensable feature in guiding the conscience of Israel's scribes and traditionists into rejecting what was false, and preserving what was truly consonant with Israel's unique faith in God. Although the prophets did not create the main lines of Israel's tradition of worship, they yet played a significant role in preserving that tradition from the decadence of the pre-exilic cult, and in shaping it to play a more formative part after the exile. The lines of development of the cult and of prophecy proceed in part together, and in part in separation. Often they touch and cross one another so that neither is really explicable without reference to the other. Early Israelite prophecy was at home in the cult, even though it was not always confined to it. Amos, Hosea and many of the great religious figures of pre-exilic prophecy found themselves forced into an opposition to the established cult of the day. Yet they all, in the form of their oracles, and in their understanding of Yahwism, betray their familiarity and partial dependence on the cultic traditions which they had inherited. After the exile prophecy returned again to its ancient home in the cultic life of the nation, but not before it had exerted a great influence upon the way in which that cultic life developed.

VI

PROPHECY AND ESCHATOLOGY

The attitude of the pre-exilic prophets to the covenant introduces us to the important question of eschatology in Israel's religion. There are two main reasons for this. Firstly the fundamental issue whether we are entitled to speak at all of an eschatology in Israel before the exile can only be decided by an examination of what the prophets had to say about the covenant. In the second place those passages in the pre-exilic prophets which have most frequently been interpreted as expressive of a positive eschatology must be examined carefully in the light of the distinctive election traditions of Israel which have exercised a formative influence upon them. This is essential whatever date we assign for the compilation of such oracles.

To begin with we must recognize the fact that the whole question of the presence or absence of eschatological ideas in the oracles of the pre-exilic prophets is one fraught with a number of difficulties. Did these messengers of Yahweh possess an eschatology, and if they did, whence did they derive it? The discussion of these questions has inevitably hinged to some extent upon the particular definition of eschatology that has been adopted. As a consequence we find recent scholars arguing both for[1] and against[2] the presence of an eschatology in pre-exilic prophecy, in a way that seems bewildering and confusing to the general reader. Such

[1] T. C. Vriezen, 'Prophecy and Eschatology', *Congress Volume, Copenhagen 1953* (SVT 1), Leiden, 1953, pp. 199ff.; E. Rohland, *Die Bedeutung der Erwählungstraditionen Israels für die Eschatologie der alttestamentlichen Propheten, passim*; E. Jenni, 'Eschatology', *IDB* II, p. 128b; J. Lindblom, 'Gibt es eine Eschatologie bei den alttestamentlichen Propheten?', *StTh* 6, 1952, pp. 79ff.; R. Hentschke, 'Gesetz und Eschatologie in der Verkündigung der Propheten', *ZEE* 4, 1960, pp. 46ff.; J. H. Grönbaek, 'Zur Frage der Eschatologie in der Verkündigung der Gerichtspropheten', *SEA* 24, 1959, pp. 5ff.; H. Graf Reventlow, *Das Amt des Propheten bei Amos*, pp. 104ff.

[2] S. Mowinckel, *He That Cometh*, pp. 126ff.; G. Fohrer, 'Die Struktur der alttestamentlichen Eschatologie', *TLZ* 85, 1960, cols. 401ff.; C. F. Whitley, *The Prophetic Achievement*, pp. 199ff.

differences, however, are more apparent than real since the argument is in large part concerned with the question, 'What is eschatology?', rather than with fundamental disagreements as to what the prophets actually taught.

It is necessary, therefore, to introduce certain general considerations of the nature of eschatology before entering upon a closer examination of the teaching of the prophets on the subject. In its narrowest sense eschatology means the doctrine of the things which concern the end of the world. In dogmatic usage, therefore, eschatology has been taken to imply the conclusion of history, and the introduction of a new and supra-historical world order. What is eschatological lies by definition on the other side of history. The fact that in certain Jewish writings, and most especially in apocalyptic, such a cosmic cataclysm is foretold, has lent a certain justification to the limitation of the term eschatology to describe such ideas. In this sense there is no eschatology in the pre-exilic prophets of the Old Testament, since the events that they are concerned with take place within history and not beyond it.[1] This definition of eschatology is, however, not only very restricted, but it does not fit the biblical material very well. It applies to a peripheral, rather than a central, feature of the Israelite hope, and has not in fact been generally adhered to in modern discussion. It is understandable therefore that in much recent biblical research it has been felt more suitable to use the term in a way which gives a much wider significance to the idea of eschatology.[2]

It is important for us, in seeking to avoid confusion, to use the term in a way which conforms to the nature of the biblical material which we wish to interpret, rather than to adhere to its etymological meaning, or to any arbitrary definition which we may wish to confer upon it. In this regard ideas of the end of the cosmos and of the cessation of history do not provide a primary biblical doctrine which can give an adequate category of interpretation. Such

[1] So especially G. Fohrer, *art. cit.*, col. 411; J. H. Grönbaek, *art. cit.*, p. 10.

[2] J. Lindblom, *art. cit.*, pp. 8off., defines eschatology by reference to the idea of two ages. Any radical change in the conditions of world order means the introduction of a new age, and may be called eschatological. T. C. Vriezen, 'Prophecy and Eschatology', *Congress Volume* (SVT 1), p. 223, uses the term eschatology to describe a faith in a new kingdom, even if there is no expectation of the destruction of the cosmos. J. H. Grönbaek, *art. cit.*, p. 10, uses the term eschatology to describe the 'conclusive aspect' of future events, so that the criterion of eschatological ideas is their finality.

ideas were introduced into Israel's hope in post-exilic times, and became most prominent in apocalyptic, which appeared quite late in Israel's religious development. They belong to the fringe, rather than to the centre, of the biblical doctrine of the divine purpose in history, which is throughout connected with the belief in God's purpose with his people Israel.[1] God's relationship to natural phenomena, in the widest sense, is less important than his relationship to people, and in particular to Israel, with whom he has a covenant. The ideas of a transformation of nature are introduced as elaborations of the belief in a new and creative work of God with his people, and developed out of the imagery of all nature's participation in the joyous return of the exiles, which Deutero-Isaiah proclaimed.[2] In consequence of this it is preferable to define eschatology in a way which allows room for this special concern with the divine relationship to Israel, and which does not obscure the intra-historical nature of such divine action.

We may, therefore, adopt a broad definition of eschatology which renders it suitable to describe the biblical ideas of God's purpose in history. Eschatology is the study of ideas and beliefs concerning the end of the present world order, and the introduction of a new order. This leaves room for two important features which generally persist in Israel's hope. These are that Yahweh's purpose with the world is bound up inextricably with his unique covenant relationship to Israel, and that his dealings with Israel take place in the arena of history. The belief in Israel's election lies at the heart of all the Old Testament promises of a new and creative work of God which is to take place in the future. We have already shown that it was a fundamental datum of the belief of the prophets that the divine world order was centralized in the special covenant existence of Israel. The prophets knew that such a covenant had come into being through historical events, which were vital to the understanding of their nation's past. The covenant, therefore, was a fact, grounded in the events of history, not based upon a timeless mythological bond between God and people. Whatever naturalistic imagery the prophets employed of a father-son relationship, or of a marriage in which Yahweh was the Bridegroom and Israel the Bride, were simply verbal pictures,

[1] Cf. E. Jenni, 'Eschatology', *IDB* II, pp. 127a, 128b.
[2] Cf. Zech. 14.6ff.; Isa. 65.17f.; 66.22; and see G. Fohrer, *art. cit.*, col. 411.

not mythological explanations of Israel's life. Such similes pointed back to the historical events of the exodus through which Israel had become the people of Yahweh, and were in no sense intended to present a mythological basis for the relationship between God and people.

If we accept this broad definition of eschatology, which we regard as most suitable to apply to the biblical material, we must proceed to consider the questions of the nature and origin of the prophetic eschatology. We have already pointed out that the primary concern of the pre-exilic canonical prophets was to foretell the coming judgment of Yahweh upon Israel. The disasters of 721 and 587 BC fulfilled these threats, and brought an end to the independent political and religious life of Israel as a nation. At the close of the exile in Babylon Deutero-Isaiah arose to assure the survivors of Israel that the time of judgment was over, and Yahweh was about to make a new beginning.[1] In Judah, after some exiles had returned, both Haggai and Zechariah took up this theme of a new coming of Yahweh in grace to restore his people, and to change their fortunes.[2] Thus with the exile it is apparent that a great change took place within the substance of the message given by those prophets whose writings have been preserved in the Old Testament. This changeover from a message predominantly of doom, to the prospect of a glorious new beginning for Israel, through the grace of Yahweh, has led several scholars to argue that eschatology only properly arose with the end of the exile.[3] At this time a new sense of hope emerged in Israelite prophecy, making it a means of encouragement and strength to the returning exiles. To make this a dividing line in the interpretation of the prophets, and their expectation of the future, has the justification that the exile clearly marks a new beginning. The judgment was past and the new age was believed to be about to dawn. None the less a study of the pre-exilic prophets shows that the hope of this new day was anticipated by them, and the promise of a new beginning of Yahweh with Israel figures in their preaching. They believed that Yahweh's grace would extend beyond the

---

[1] Isa. 40.1ff., etc.

[2] Hag. 1.8; 2.6–9; Zech. 1.14ff.; 2.14ff. (EVV 10ff.); 8.1ff.

[3] S. Mowinckel, *He That Cometh*, pp. 133ff.; G. Fohrer, 'Die Struktur der alttestamentlichen Eschatologie', *TLZ* 85, 1960, cols. 401ff.

fearful judgment which they saw as about to fall. Consequently we may argue that the pre-exilic prophets of Israel did possess an eschatology.

Before we can consider the nature and origin of this eschatology, however, it is valuable to examine the popular hopes that existed in Israel before the time of Amos. It is apparent from what he had to say that the people whom he addressed did cling to certain very optimistic ideas about the future of their nation:

> Woe to you who desire the day of Yahweh!
>   Why would you have the day of Yahweh?
> It is darkness, and not light;
>   as if a man fled from a lion,
>   and a bear met him;
> or went into the house and leaned with his hand against the wall,
>   and a snake bit him.
> Is not the day of Yahweh darkness, and not light,
>   and gloom with no brightness in it?
>
> (Amos 5.18–20.)

A considerable amount of argument has centred upon the conception of the Day of Yahweh which is evidenced here. It is contested whether it originally referred to a celebration of an event in the cult,[1] or to an event drawn from the ideas connected with the holy war.[2] S. Mowinckel's interpretation of this Day of Yahweh as referring to the recurring New Year's Day of the Autumn Festival, celebrating Yahweh's Enthronement, meant that such a day was a cultic celebration, not an eschatological *dénouement* of Yahweh's purpose in history. It was simply the day which marked the renewal of blessing from Yahweh, as this was anticipated in the major festival of the Israelite calendar. This festival itself, however, proclaimed to Israel the coming of a blessing which was more than simply the renewal of natural life and fertility. It foretold the coming of Yahweh to judge the nations, and to establish his righteous rule upon earth. Just how it was conceived and

---

[1] S. Mowinckel, *Psalmenstudien* II, pp. 228ff. Certain important modifications of Mowinckel's earlier interpretation are expressed in *The Psalms in Israel's Worship* I, pp. 189ff.

[2] G. von Rad, 'The Origin of the Concept of the Day of Yahweh', *JSS* 4, 1959, pp. 97ff.; *Theologie des A.T.* II, pp. 133ff. Cf. also H. Wheeler Robinson, *Inspiration and Revelation in the Old Testament*, Oxford, 1946, pp. 135ff., for a discussion of the problems concerning the subject.

celebrated in Bethel we do not know,[1] but in Jerusalem, for which the Psalter provides a valuable witness, it was not only the day which marked the annual renewal of the cycle of nature, but such a renewal pointing forward to the historical fulfilment of the promises of Yahweh to Israel.[2] Thus the distinctively Israelite recognition of the nation's origins in Yahweh's providential ordering of history lent a historical and forward-looking aspect to its understanding of the Autumn Festival. The New Year's Day was the Day of Yahweh which anticipated the completion of the divine will for Israel. In the age of the Davidic-Solomonic empire it is probable that such a hope was in large measure thought to be fulfilled, but with the break-up of that empire at Solomon's death, it appears that a sense of the incompleteness of Yahweh's purpose for Israel became widespread. This attitude was taken up in the cult, so that the final great Day of Yahweh was regarded as still in the future, in which all nations would acknowledge the sovereignty of Yahweh. This forward-looking aspect of the Autumn Festival became a vital, and characteristically Israelite feature of its liturgy and mood. It expressed in its hymns and rites much of the tradition of Yahweh's great saving acts of Israel's past, with the idea of a goal to which these were leading. Thus it was imbued with the notion that Yahweh was working out a purpose within history. It was not, therefore, simply a day which recurred each year, and which marked a turning-point in the annual cycle of life and renewal. The Day of Yahweh which was celebrated in Israel's New Year Festival was thought to point forward to the day when Yahweh would carry to completion his purposes for his people.

This deeper understanding of the character of Israel's cult, and the element of hope which it proclaimed, has corrected the somewhat one-sided perspective of the claim that the Day of Yahweh was a cultic event. Whilst this is true, it is apparent that Israel's cult was thoroughly imbued with a sense of hope and anticipation

[1] Cf. G. Widengren, *Sakrales Königtum im Alten Testament und im Judentum*, Stuttgart, 1955, pp. 34ff., who finds in the Samaritan liturgy evidence of an earlier royal rite which he believes derives from the celebration of the Autumn Festival at Bethel. For a criticism of Widengren's view see S. Mowinckel, *He That Cometh*, p. 72 note.

[2] Cf. A. R. Johnson, *Sacral Kingship in Ancient Israel*, p. 54 note; and S. Mowinckel, *The Psalms in Israel's Worship* I, pp. 186ff., 191; II, pp. 231f.; *He That Cometh*, pp. 132f.

for the future, deriving from the knowledge of Yahweh's election of Israel, and his will to fulfil the promises made in the covenant. Yahweh's plans for his people were expected to attain their goal through the historical vindication of Israel, and were not limited to the outpouring of blessing in the cult. The suggestion that the idea of the Day of Yahweh contained ideas derived from the institution of the holy war,[1] in which Yahweh was expected to lead the armies of Israel to victory over the nations, is not without value, and a measure of truth.

The popular hope of the Israelite cult looked for the coming of the Day of Yahweh, and the great New Year's Day of the Autumn Festival was a promise of the advent of this day. The crowning day of Israel's festival calendar anticipated the triumphant day when Yahweh's purposes for Israel would be fulfilled, when his kingdom would be established, and when he would secure justice and prosperity for his people. The cult did not promise everything here and now, but was itself influenced by the Israelite belief in a dialectic of promise and fulfilment running through the nation's history. In the light of this element of prophetic promise which the Enthronement Festival of Yahweh proclaimed, we can see the essential features of the popular hope of Israel, and can understand their relationship to the cult. In its Jerusalem form this festival was closely related to the belief in the divine election of Mount Zion, and Yahweh's covenant with David.[2] It was therefore in this way that the particular cult-traditions of Jerusalem were related to the Israelite hope, and were woven into the fabric of the Israelite expectation of ultimate greatness. For political reasons it is clear that such Judean elements were absent in Bethel, where Amos appeared.

This popular expectation of the Day of Yahweh provided the people and their festivities with an attitude of easy-going optimism, which greatly incensed Amos when he saw how little it was concerned with moral and spiritual realities. Consequently he proclaimed that the Day of Yahweh's triumph would be a disaster

[1] G. von Rad, 'The Origin of the Concept of the Day of Yahweh', *JSS* 4, 1959, *passim*, and in *Theologie des A.T.* II, pp. 133ff.

[2] The interpretation of the Jerusalem Autumn Festival as a royal Zion festival is particularly advocated by H. J. Kraus, *Die Königsherrschaft Gottes im Alten Testament, passim*; cf. also his *Psalmen* I, pp. 197ff., 342ff.; II, pp. 879ff.; and *Gottesdienst in Israel* (2 Aufl.), pp. 215ff.

for the nation, because Yahweh's judgment would mean the end of sinful Israel. Amos therefore broke with the popular hope, which the cult affirmed. Its facile expectation of Israel's exaltation and triumph had lost any connexion with the moral demands of the covenant.

Amos proclaimed a judgment which would entail the breaking-off of the bond between Yahweh and his people. In this threat of the dissolution of the covenant Amos was interpreting the curse of the law in a new and radical way, which compelled him to declare a future for Israel of a totally different kind from that anticipated by the cult.[1] Yet in doing this Amos could claim to be the true spokesman of the covenant, even whilst opposing the hopes and expectations which the popular mind associated with it. He was taking the covenant seriously, whilst the cult did not.

It is plain therefore that Amos and the other pre-exilic prophets did not derive their eschatology from the optimistic promises of the cult, for their preaching marks a very radical break with such popular hopes. The future that loomed before Israel, as they saw it, was a disastrous judgment, which would annihilate the nation. Only because this threat of judgment was itself rooted in the cultic proclamation of the law can we claim that some connexion existed between Israel's cult and the eschatology of the pre-exilic prophets. Throughout their preaching these prophets expressed a similar message of condemnation and punishment. It is an eschatology of doom, in which the existing order between Yahweh and Israel was threatened with extinction. Is it possible then that at the same time such prophets could also have believed in a happier future for Israel?

It is clear that Hosea, at least, did believe that such a future was possible, since he pictures a time when Yahweh would begin afresh to create a new Israel. He pictures the new nation as a bride, taken back to the wilderness, where the marriage bond with Yahweh was first sealed:

> Therefore, behold, I will allure her,
> and bring her into the wilderness,
> and speak tenderly to her.

[1] Cf. R. Hentschke, 'Gesetz und Eschatologie in der Verkündigung der Propheten', *ZEE* 4, 1960, pp. 46ff., 54, who argues that the basis of Amos's eschatology of doom is to be found in his radical interpretation of the curse of the law. Cf. also W. Zimmerli, 'Das Gesetz im Alten Testament', *Gottes Offenbarung*, pp. 270ff., and *Das Gesetz und die Propheten*, pp. 81ff.

And there I will give her her vineyards,
    And make the Valley of Achor a door of hope.
And there she shall answer as in the days of her youth,
    as at the time when she came out of the land of Egypt.
(Hos. 2.16–17 [EVV 14–15]; cf. 2.18–25 [EVV 16–23].)

Afterward the children of Israel shall return and seek Yahweh their God,[1] and they shall come in fear to Yahweh and to his goodness in future days. (Hos. 3.5; cf. 11.8–9; 14.5–9 [EVV 4–8].)

Hosea is here asserting that Yahweh's judgment would not be the end of Israel, since the covenant was founded on the divine love, and that love would persevere, and begin again with the task of establishing a people of God. What Hosea envisaged was a new desert sojourn, and a new occupation of the land, but this time without the corrupting influence of Canaan. Hosea's hope for Israel's future was conceived in terms of a renewal of the exodus tradition as the supreme evidence of the grace of Yahweh. Israel would be re-elected by a new act of salvation.

It has been necessary to begin with Hosea rather than Amos in this consideration of the hope of the re-establishment of Israel, since the latter's utterance on the subject has often been regarded as unauthentic. His prophecies contain an oracle which speaks of the restoration of the power and authority of the Davidic dynasty:

In that day I will raise up the tent of David that is fallen
    and repair its breaches,
    and raise up its ruins,
    and rebuild it as in the days of old;
that they may possess the remnant of Edom
    and all the nations who are called by my name,
        says Yahweh who does this. (Amos 9.11–12.)

This oracle has frequently been denied to Amos, and has been regarded as a later, post-exilic, addition to his prophecies, which alleviated the unremitting insistence upon judgment. Its authenticity has, however, found strong defenders in recent study,[2] and

---

[1] The words 'and David their king' are accepted by most commentators as a subsequent (Judean) gloss. See above p. 49.
[2] E. Rohland, *op. cit.*, pp. 59, 231f.; G. von Rad, *Theologie des A.T.* II, pp. 148f.; H. Graf Reventlow, *Das Amt des Propheten bei Amos*, pp. 91ff. Graf Reventlow also seeks to defend the authenticity of verses 13–15 of Amos 9, which form a separate oracle, by relating them to the blessing ritual of the covenant cult, which, he believes, provided the form Amos has adopted here (*op. cit.*, pp. 94ff.).

it may be understood to refer, not to the eclipse of the Davidic dynasty and kingdom with the exile, but to the division and disruption of the Davidic empire after Solomon's death. What Amos had in mind was the ending of the division into two separate kingdoms of Israel and Judah, by their return to one united kingdom under a Davidic head. As a Judean Amos thought of Israel's future happiness in terms of the Jerusalem-David tradition. No compelling reason exists, therefore, for denying this oracle to Amos, or for discounting the claim that Amos did entertain a hope for his people's future, which lay on the far side of the judgment which was about to fall. For him the re-election of the Davidic dynasty, and the re-establishing of the old Davidic kingdom, represented a renewal of Yahweh's grace to Israel, and the expectation of a new beginning.

In this proclamation of a renewed work of Yahweh with Israel, after the judgment, we can see how the older expectations and promises of the cult were taken up. The hopes associated with Jerusalem and the covenant between Yahweh and David were projected into the future and their fulfilment was looked for after the judgment of Yahweh had fallen upon the existing nation. Amos has interposed his own radical condemnation of the present order, and the threat of its dissolution, between the election of David and the goal of Yahweh's promises to him. Just as Hosea certainly proclaimed a positive eschatology of the renewal of Israel by a new act of divine election as at the exodus, so also the prophecies of the restoration of the Davidic empire contained in the last chapter of Amos, may well be an authentic utterance of the prophet.

We find this adoption and reinterpretation of the old election traditions still further in evidence when we consider the preaching of other prophets, who foretold the doom of the exile. Both Isaiah and Micah promised the eventual vindication of the greatness of Jerusalem,[1] and the glories of the new ruler who would sit upon David's throne.[2] This latter promise was also reiterated by Jeremiah[3] and Ezekiel.[4] Yet the attention of both these prophets was primarily upon the rebirth of Israel as a nation, rather than upon the eventual fulfilment of the promises to David. Jeremiah spoke

[1] Isa. 2.2–4; (= Micah 4.1–4).
[2] Isa. 8.23ff. (EVV 9.1ff.); 11.1ff.; Micah 5.1ff. (EVV 2ff.).
[3] Jer. 23.5f.   [4] Ezek. 34.23ff.; 37.15ff.

of a new covenant,[1] when Yahweh would restore the shattered fortunes of Israel by taking them again to himself as his people. The fact that it was the law which had brought disaster upon the first Israel is evidenced by Jeremiah's concern for a new work of Yahweh in the heart of every Israelite:

> But this is the covenant which I will make with the house of Israel after those days, says Yahweh: I will put my law within them, and I will write it upon their hearts; and I will be their God, and they shall be my people.
>
> (Jer. 31.33; cf. Ezek. 36.26f.)

It is discernible that Jeremiah felt a certain problem and frustration with the law of the covenant. The assurance that the renewed Israel would not be as faithless and erring as the old could only be found in the hope of a new attitude brought about by Yahweh. Whilst Jeremiah knew that the law was a gift of Yahweh's grace, he knew also that it was the curse of the law that had brought disaster on the nation in his own lifetime. He came to believe that Israel's only defence against the threatening aspect of the law was to be found in an inner change of heart wrought by God. Yahweh must not only give the law, but also the power to obey it. Ezekiel foretold the restoration of Israel in terms of a resurrection of the dead nation.[2] There was to be a new migration into Canaan, and a new occupation of its cities and villages.

The pre-exilic prophets did, therefore, possess an eschatology, but it was an eschatology governed by the realization that the people to whom they preached were under the sentence of death. The existing order was threatened with destruction, and the prophets understood this threat by the radical interpretation which they gave to the curse of the law proclaimed in the cult. They were compelled, consequently, to make a complete break with the optimistic promises of the cult. Yet beyond the judgment they were led to declare that Yahweh would re-elect and re-establish his people, and they prophesied the coming of these events in terms of the old election traditions of Israel.[3] Their hope for the future was

---

[1] Jer. 31.31ff.   [2] Ezek. 37.1ff.; cf. 36.8ff.; 37.15ff.

[3] It is the major thesis of E. Rohland's study, *Die Bedeutung der Erwählungstraditionen Israels für die Eschatologie der alttestamentlichen Propheten*, that the different election traditions of Israel form the material out of which the eschatology of the prophets was formed. This occurred when the old covenant order was threatened with extinction, and the prophets looked to Yahweh for a new beginning of Israel. See especially *op. cit.*, pp. 266ff.

not of a progressive improvement of the situation in which Israel found itself, but of a radical new beginning, when the old order had been judged and brought to an end. It is because this expectation meant the ending of the existing order, and the breaking-in of a new, divinely created, order, that we may justifiably call this an eschatology, even though these events were to take place within history, and not beyond it.

It was this expectation of a renewal of Israel, after the doom of judgment and exile, which formed the main line of development for Israel's eschatological hope. This did not derive from the popular notions of God-given blessing, centred in the cultic expectation of the Day of Yahweh, but in a promise of God's action to restore his covenant people. The Israelite eschatological hope, therefore, arose out of the attitude to the covenant, in judgment and promise, of the pre-exilic canonical prophets. It directly concerned the experience of the exile and the hope of restoration which lay beyond. In this hope of restoration, the old election traditions of Israel provided, not only a stock of imagery, but also a pattern and a foundation to which the prophets could appeal. It was natural, therefore, that in their pictures of the future happiness of the people of God, the prophets should have made use of much of the language, and many of the ideas, of the popular hope.

The full flowering of the prophetic eschatology came with the appearance of Deutero-Isaiah, the opening of whose prophecies declare that the time of judgment is past, and that Yahweh is about to do a new thing for Israel. This new work was to take the form of a triumphant return of the exiles from Babylon, in which all nature was expected to co-operate by preparing the way for the exiles to make their perilous journey.[1] Amongst the exiled Jews the time of suffering was shortly to draw to an end, and a new journey through the desert would begin, and would find its climax in the arrival home of the Jews in Jerusalem. Yahweh himself would lead this triumphant company,[2] in what was envisaged as a new exodus.[3] In fact the prophet's hearers are bidden to forget the

[1] Isa. 40.3ff.; 41.17ff.; 43.1ff., 14ff.; 44.1ff., 24ff.; 49.8ff.; 51.1ff., 9ff.; 52.7ff.
[2] Isa. 52.12.
[3] Cf. esp. Isa. 51.9–10; 52.11–12; 48.20–21. See B. W. Anderson, 'Exodus Typology in Second Isaiah', *Israel's Prophetic Heritage*, ed. Anderson and Harrelson, pp. 177ff.; W. Zimmerli, 'Der "neue Exodus" in der Verkündigung der beiden grossen Exilspropheten', *Gottes Offenbarung*, pp. 192ff.

former things, because what Yahweh is about to do will be a new thing.[1] By these 'former things' the prophet was referring to the whole earlier history of Israel, extending from the exodus to the exile.[2] This is now a closed epoch so far as the prophet is concerned, and the new beginning which Yahweh is about to make will far exceed it in glory. The return to Jerusalem was to be the signal for a great transformation of the existing social and political conditions of the world. Jerusalem was to become the spiritual centre to which all nations would make pilgrimage, bringing their tribute-offerings with them.[3] In Deutero-Isaiah we encounter an extraordinary blending of the exodus and Zion traditions. These no longer stand side by side, as was the case in Jeremiah and Ezekiel, but are woven together so that the glorifying of Jerusalem is to be the goal of the new exodus and the new occupation of the land. The rebuilding of the temple and of the new Jerusalem were to be attained by the direct intervention of Yahweh in historical events.[4] One important feature, amidst the many remarkable aspects of this reminting of Israel's hope, concerns the reinterpretation of the covenant with the house of David.[5] No longer is this referred to the Davidic house alone, but to all the survivors of the Israelite nation. These are to be the recipients of the covenant-mercies of David in the future. Henceforth it is the nation as a whole, and not simply the family of David, who are to be the heirs of Yahweh's covenant promise to the great king. No individual 'messianic' figure is expected to occupy the Davidic throne since the entire nation has become heir to the ancient royal promises.

---

[1] Isa. 41.21–29; 42.8–9; 43.9, 16–19; 44.6–8; 45.9–13, 20–21; 46.9–11; 48.3ff.

[2] So E. Rohland, *op. cit.*, pp. 99f., against C. R. North, 'The "Former Things" and the "New Things" in Deutero-Isaiah', *Studies in Old Testament Prophecy*, ed. H. H. Rowley, pp. 111ff., who interprets most references to these 'former things' of events of the relatively recent past, and in particular of the earlier victories of Cyrus. This is so for 41.22; 42.9; 43.9; 48.3. In 43.8 and perhaps 46.9–11, North thinks the exodus may have been in mind. Cf. also B. W. Anderson, 'Exodus Typology in Second Isaiah', pp. 187f., who argues that the 'former things' are the events of Israel's *heilsgeschichte*, pre-eminently the old exodus.

[3] Isa. 49.12f.; 55.5.

[4] Isa. 44.28.

[5] Isa. 55.1–5. Cf. especially on this section O. Eissfeldt, 'The Promises of Grace to David in Isaiah 55.1–5', *Israel's Prophetic Heritage*, ed. Anderson and Harrelson, pp. 196ff.

A further feature in this prophetic reinterpretation of the old Israelite traditions is to be found in the way in which the language and ideas of the pre-exilic Enthronement Festival are taken up and applied to the forthcoming historical events. The kingship of Yahweh would not be the subject of a cultic celebration, as it had been in former days, but a universal revelation of his power, made known through the historical events centring in the return of the exiles to Jerusalem. The pre-exilic cult of Jerusalem provided the prophet with a stock of imagery and language which he used to express in a remarkably powerful way the eschatological drama which he foretold as about to take place.[1] In this respect, although we cannot argue that the prophetic eschatology was derived from the cult, it is apparent that the language and imagery in which that eschatological hope was clothed did borrow from earlier cultic material. This is true also of Deutero-Isaiah's assurances of salvation, which are couched in a form which originally belonged to the cult, wherein the priest gave assurance to the worshipper of his acceptance by Yahweh.[2]

This impressive phenomenon, which we encounter in Deutero-Isaiah, of the reinterpretation of ideas which at one time belonged to the pre-exilic festivals and services of the Jerusalem temple, cannot be unrelated to the formal cessation of the Jerusalem cult. Although it is clear that not all worship ceased on the site where the ruins of the temple lay,[3] much of the old cultus must have been discontinued, and many of the nation's leading figures were separated from it in exile.[4] Deutero-Isaiah was himself among

[1] S. Mowinckel, *Psalmenstudien* II, pp. 256f.; *He That Cometh*, pp. 139ff.; *The Psalms in Israel's Worship* I, pp. 189ff. The alternative view, that the ideas of Yahweh's enthronement, as expressed in the Psalms, were derived from Deutero-Isaiah, cannot now be accepted. It is advocated by N. H. Snaith, *The Jewish New Year Festival*, London, 1947, pp. 200f., 206f.; H. J. Kraus, *Die Königsherrschaft Gottes im Alten Testament*, pp. 99ff.

[2] J. Begrich, 'Das priesterliche Heilsorakel', *ZAW* 52, 1934, pp. 81ff.; *Studien zu Deuterojesaja*, rep. Munich, 1963, pp. 14ff.

[3] Cf. Jer. 41.5. That sacrificial worship did cease in 586 BC for a considerable interval, with important consequences for Israel's religion, is argued by D. R. Jones, 'The Cessation of Sacrifice after the Destruction of the Temple in 586 BC', *JTS* (NS) 14, 1963, pp. 12ff.

[4] E. Janssen, *Juda in der Exilszeit. Ein Beitrag zur Frage der Entstehung des Judentums* (FRLANT 69), Göttingen, 1956 pp. 58ff., stresses that whilst not all cultic and spiritual life ceased in Juda, the destruction of the temple became a problem for faith.

these exiles, and his particular reinterpretation of the material of the old festival calendar could only have arisen as a result of a prolonged consideration of the significance of such rites. The collapse of the old cultic order, with its long-established traditions and continuity, was the opportunity for a fresh and stimulating reapplication of its ideas. The hopes and promises which had once been nurtured in the cult of the Jerusalem temple were now lifted out of their earlier setting, and used to describe Israel's great hope of the rebirth of their national and spiritual life. The events of history, which Deutero-Isaiah saw as imminent, would carry to fulfilment the eschatological dream of a new Israel.

In a great many ways the oracles of Deutero-Isaiah mark a significant change in Israelite prophecy. The eschatological content, pointing to a new and glorious manifestation of divine power in the rebirth of Israel, stands at the centre of the prophet's thought. This new election and new wilderness journey were expected to be crowned by a triumphant homecoming of the exiles to Jerusalem, which all the nations would witness, and acknowledge as the work of Yahweh. The period of the divine wrath was believed to have passed, since Israel had accepted its judgment, and now the nation stood at the brink of a new beginning. The salvation that was about to dawn was promised as the work of Yahweh's grace, and underlying it we sense the conviction that only Yahweh could make Israel fit to be his people. Of its own self Israel was not capable of fulfilling the will imposed upon it by the covenant.

The actual circumstances of the return from Babylon did not match the glory which Deutero-Isaiah had anticipated, and the arrival of the homecoming exiles in Jerusalem was not greeted by any universal homage to Israel. In the disappointment of the difficult times, when the handful of returned Jews endeavoured to recommence a normal life in Jerusalem, the eschatological hope became a problem. Why had it not been fulfilled? Both Haggai and Zechariah took up afresh the theme of Yahweh's near arrival in glory to raise Israel to the headship of the nations. Haggai urged the rebuilding of the temple that Yahweh might appear in it in glory.[1] Zechariah encouraged the people with the promise that soon Yahweh would re-elect Jerusalem, and would dwell in its midst.[2]

[1] Hag. 1.7f.   [2] Zech. 2.14–16 (EVV 10–12); cf. 8.3.

In the prophecies of Malachi we have a reawakening of censure upon Israel for its sins, especially as these concern the neglect of the cult.[1] As in the pre-exilic prophets there has arisen again the sense that Israel is not ready for Yahweh to come to it in fulfilment of his promises.[2] A new purging of Israel must be undergone before Yahweh could fulfil the promise of his coming, and of the nation's glory. The later chapters of Zechariah (9–14) take up afresh many of the themes of the ancient cult-festivals of Israel, and work them into a picture of the nation's hope. When Old Testament prophecy came to its end there was still the awareness of unfulfilled promises. Still the eyes of the prophets were upon the future, looking for the creation of the New Israel, with a new covenant and a new dwelling of God within Israel's midst.

We may summarize the conclusions of this chapter in the following way. The eschatology of the Old Testament prophets is primarily concerned with the future of Israel as the covenant people of Yahweh. In reacting against the popular optimism of the expectation of the Day of Yahweh, the pre-exilic prophets foretold that Israel would be judged and the covenant brought to an end. Yet beyond this judgment they pointed also to a new beginning when Israel would be reborn, and would become once again the people of the covenant. The old election traditions were used by the prophets to portray the re-election of Israel, and the new covenant which Yahweh would make with them. The ancient covenant promises were now expected to find their fulfilment when the judgment was passed, and a new beginning made. In particular the promises to the Davidic dynasty, and the glorification of Mount Zion in the cult, became themes which expressed the greatness and splendour which Yahweh would give to Israel. With Deutero-Isaiah there came the assertion that the judgment was passed, and that Yahweh was about to create a new Israel out of the survivors of the old nation in exile. After the return, when the promises were not immediately fulfilled, disappointment gave way to a more patient anticipation of the coming of Yahweh. An eschatological hope of the New Israel, with a New Jerusalem, blessed by the presence of Yahweh, became a prominent feature of post-exilic Judaism. The last of the canonical prophets still points towards the expectation of Yahweh's triumphant coming to his people.

[1] Mal. 1.6ff.; 2.1ff., 13ff.   [2] Mal. 3.1ff., 19ff. (EVV 4.1ff.).

VII

CONCLUSION

THIS short study of the canonical prophets in the Old Testament has been concerned to show their relationship with the covenant between Yahweh and Israel. It has of necessity not been possible within this compass to provide a detailed examination of the teaching of each of the prophets, or to attempt an overall assessment of the significance of prophecy for the study of religion in general. In particular we have avoided any consideration of the psychological basis of prophetic inspiration, which has occupied much of the attention of scholars since the important work of G. Hölscher. Our concern has been, not with the persons of the prophets themselves, but with the message which they gave. There are two aspects of modern study of the Old Testament which have particularly influenced our approach. These are the importance of the cult in Israelite religion, and the contributions of form-criticism and tradition-history towards an understanding of the history of the Old Testament literature. In the latter case it is the application of form-criticism to the prophetic writings which has been relevant to our purpose. These two aspects are not unrelated to each other, since it was largely in the cult that forms of prophetic utterance were developed, and it was also from the rites and festivals of Israelite worship that the prophets frequently borrowed their language and imagery.

This recent interest in Israel's worship and in the part played by that worship as a vehicle of tradition, has illuminated very clearly the importance of the covenant concept in Israel's life. The controlling factor in the variety of Israel's religious traditions was their overall concern with the covenant by which Israel had become the people of Yahweh. The cultic celebrations of Israel, organized in a festival calendar, were responsible for maintaining a right understanding of Yahweh's relationship to them. Most especially was this so in regard to the Autumn Festival, which held a particular significance as an act of reaffirmation and renewal of the covenant. As a consequence the tradition of the covenant, in a recollection of the history of its origin and of its laws, constituted Israel's knowledge of Yahweh. There was little interest in speculating about the being of Yahweh, as he was in himself, but instead a concern to remember how and why Israel stood under the lordship of Yahweh. The people were taught to see themselves as the recipients of Yahweh's grace, made known in the deliverance of their ancestors from slavery in Egypt. They were summoned to respond by obedience to the covenant laws delivered to them on Mount Sinai.

The earliest prophets of Israel stood within this covenant tradition of worship. They accepted and upheld it, and many of them functioned as authorized members of the cultic personnel. The task of all the prophets was to care for the true welfare of Israel by intercession for the nation, and by the procuring of oracles for all who sought them. They prophesied both blessing and woe, as the circumstances required, just as the covenant cult proclaimed both blessings and curses for the obedient and disobedient respectively. They were therefore accepted preachers of judgment as well as salvation. This threat of Yahweh's wrath concerned sinners both within and without the ranks of the nation. For the obedient in Israel the prophets held out promises of the continuance and increase of the blessing of Yahweh.

The appearance of Amos marked a sudden and important change in this pattern of prophetic preaching. Whilst, as a prophet, Amos aligned himself within the circle of Yahweh's messengers, he knew that the judgment he was called upon to announce was not merely a purging of Israel from its sinful elements, but meant the end of the covenant relationship between Yahweh and Israel. The form of a judgment-oracle against an individual was turned into a judgment-oracle against the nation. As the mediator of the divine word to Israel he could no longer stand within the covenant order to prop it up, but had to step outside it to announce its end. It was therefore not simply that Amos preached judgment, which singled him out from his predecessors, but the fact that the judgment which he preached meant the breaking-off of Yahweh's unique relationship to Israel. In this Amos was heard to say something new and fearful, which gave a new impact to his insistence upon the ethical demands of the covenant, and which marked a new departure in Israel's religious life. It was this unique content of his preaching that has led to the fact that written prophecy begins with Amos. We may claim therefore that the significance of Amos is to be found in his attitude to the covenant tradition of Israel. The vindication of such a message of doom by the events of history, when the Northern Kingdom suffered defeat and exile in 721 BC, added further weight to his words. In many respects Amos belonged to the line of the earlier *nĕbhī'īm*, yet the range of his message carried him beyond them. That Amos ever functioned as a cultic official is unlikely, and he seems rather to have associated himself with the numerous prophets who remained free of any permanent attachment to one sanctuary. Hosea too foretold the end of the Northern Kingdom, whilst in the South, Isaiah, Micah and others continued the tradition of warning the people of an impending doom.

The examination of the traditions of Israel's election, to which the pre-exilic prophets appealed in their preaching, shows that for them the central fact of Israel's existence was the deliverance by Yahweh of their ancestors from Egypt. This was an election of grace, ratified by the covenant to which it led, and crowned by the gift of the land of Canaan. The three themes of exodus, desert sojourn and conquest form the central core of Israel's faith in its divine calling and made up the tradition of the covenant. This Sinai covenant tradition is the ultimate basis of appeal for Amos, Hosea, Jeremiah and Ezekiel. In Judah this covenant tradition was extended and altered by the addition of a belief in the election by Yahweh of the house of David, and of Mount Zion, which carried the theme of conquest up to the age of David and the formation of the Israelite State. Thus the older covenant tradition of the Israelite amphictyony was subsumed by a new covenant ideology centring in the divine election of David and of Mount Zion. In the court circles of Jerusalem, therefore, there grew up a political theology which radically altered, and partly replaced, the earlier amphictyonic religion of Israel. The sacral kingship ideology, coupled with the cult of the temple, introduced a great many innovations, and, of necessity, suppressed some features of the earlier faith. Yet the two traditions were never wholly independent, and much of the Sinai covenant religion continued to be a strong influence in Judah. We cannot therefore draw the conclusion that because the prophets Isaiah and Micah make little reference to the exodus-Sinai events they were either ignorant of them, or regarded them as of little importance. They were presupposed in the tradition of the Davidic covenant, and were present in the cult of Jerusalem, both of which were factors of the utmost importance for these prophets. Zephaniah also shows a strong attachment to the particular traditions of Zion. It is not difficult to see why this Jerusalem-centred political theology, with its divine support for the Davidic dynasty, was rejected in the Northern Kingdom of Israel, after the disruption under Jeroboam. The use made by the pre-exilic prophets of these election traditions shows that they were concerned to remind Israel of the grace wherein it stood, and to base their allegations of disloyalty and disobedience upon this fact. The offence of Israel was to have received the call of Yahweh, and to have rejected it. Its punishment in consequence was to be disowned by Yahweh and scattered among the nations.

The attitude to the law in the pre-exilic prophets is closely governed by a concern with it as an expression of the demands imposed upon Israel by the covenant. Evidence of Israel's disregard of this law the prophets found in the prevalent injustice and immorality of the nation's life. The social and religious leaders of the nation had failed in their duties and had allowed the injunctions of the covenant to fall into neglect. In consequence of this breakdown in Israelite social and religious life, the prophets stood in the place of Yahweh to call to judgment his erring people. They placed a new insistence upon the ethical demands of the covenant, and interpreted in a radical way the curse of the law.

The breakdown in the tradition and maintenance of Israel's covenant law was related to the failure of the cult to maintain the Yahwistic tradition, since the law should have been preserved and declared in the cultic ceremonies. Through its variety, and its indiscriminate borrowings from Canaan, the cult had become a very uncertain witness to the true nature and will of Yahweh. Only in isolated groups and communities was the authentic Israelite tradition preserved. Among these groups the companies of prophets must have had an important place, as also did the

communities of Levites. The pre-exilic prophets owed a considerable debt to these circles of faithful Israelites, who kept alive many
vital elements of the nation's religious heritage. The attacks by the
canonical prophets upon the sanctuaries and their priests were
motivated by a consciousness of this failure of the cult to preserve
the true knowledge of Yahweh. In the prophetic writings we find
an opposition to the cult and its institutions which marks a great
departure from the attitude of the earlier *nĕbhî'îm* who had worked
in close association with the sanctuaries. This opposition to the
sanctuaries and their sacrificial cult was linked to the claim of the
prophets to be the true spokesmen of the covenant. The cult was
condemned because it had failed to remain true to its purpose of
bearing witness to Yahweh, and of being a channel of communication and blessing between Israel and him. The prophets actualized
the covenant tradition in a situation of crisis, in which the old
order had fallen into decay. In the eventual outcome, after the
disasters of defeat and exile, the influence of these prophetic
criticisms upon the development of Israel's worship was considerable. The survivors of the cult-personnel found themselves
compelled, by the judgments of Yahweh in history, to revise their
own particular traditions to ensure that they accorded more
closely with the spiritual demands of the covenant. The attitude of
the pre-exilic prophets to Israel's worship, therefore, only finds its
fullest explanation in the light of the attitude of both to the
covenant.

One of the most vexed of all questions in the interpretation of
the Old Testament has concerned the eschatology of the prophets
and the place of its origin. It has become a matter of debate
whether the pre-exilic prophets possessed an eschatology at all.
Such arguments are partly occasioned by an uncertainty of
terminology, so that whether we admit, or deny, the presence
of eschatological ideas, may not betoken any great difference of
opinion as to what the prophets actually said. If we relate eschatology to the idea of the covenant, which is of primary importance
for Israelite religion, then the threat of the ending of the present
covenant relationship, and the promise of a new act of divine
election, may be termed eschatological. In this sense we may claim
that an eschatology is to be found in the pre-exilic prophets of
Israel. In their preaching the declaration of Yahweh's ending of

his covenant with Israel was coupled with the promise that after-
wards a new beginning would be made. This was proclaimed in
terms of a new election and a new covenant in which the traditions
of the old covenant order were taken up, and reinterpreted of the
future. The eschatology of the pre-exilic prophets arose therefore
out of their consciousness that the covenant people stood under
the divine judgment. Nevertheless beyond this coming doom they
looked for the time when Yahweh would begin afresh with Israel.
The frustration and failure of the first election would be the
occasion for a new election and a new covenant. The promises
which the covenant contained, especially those which centred
around the glorifying of Jerusalem and the Davidic dynasty, were
projected into the future as images of the future bliss.

This brief summary of our conclusions enables us to provide
some kind of assessment of the place of the canonical prophets in
Israel's religious history, and to consider their importance for Old
Testament theology. Primarily the significance of the canonical
prophets is to be found in the part which they played in maintaining and interpreting the Yahwistic tradition through years of
crisis. Their unique contribution to Israel's faith was to have
actualized the covenant tradition in the days of its obscurity and
loss. At the same time they reacted creatively upon this tradition,
which they received only in a fragmentary form, and made it into
something fresh and powerful so that it could again enrich Israel's
life. The Yahwistic tradition existed before Amos, and prophecy
itself had a long and significant history before his time, yet Amos
introduced something so startlingly new that later generations
treasured the record of his preaching and activity. This novelty
consisted in Amos's insistence that Yahweh was Lord of his
covenant with Israel, and that the threats as well as the promises
which the covenant proclaimed, were real, because Yahweh was
the living God. Prophecy rose to a new level with Amos because
he spoke not simply to sustain the covenant, but to uphold a
right understanding of what the covenant demanded, and the
fearful consequences of disobedience. After Amos there arose a
notable succession of prophets who delivered a similar message of
doom upon a sinful Israel. In the light of history, when first in
721 BC the Northern Kingdom fell, and then subsequently Judah also
experienced disaster and exile in 587 BC, these prophecies of doom

were seen to have been fulfilled. The old order of Israel was seen to have collapsed, and the meaning of that collapse, as the will of Yahweh, could only be found by heeding the prophetic interpretation of it. Such prophecy provided a theodicy of Yahweh's dealings with his people. That here, and not in the false optimism of the cult, or of the 'false' prophets, was to be found the true word of Yahweh was now made plain. Amos, and those who followed in his succession, had shown themselves to be the true spokesmen of the covenant. In the ultimate analysis it is a consequence of this particular concern with the covenant, and its historical fortunes, that led to the retention and preservation by Israel's traditionists of such prophecies. The intrinsic value of the message, and its historical vindication, were essential features in the eventual formation of a prophetic corpus of writings, and ultimately of their being accorded canonical status. Both intrinsic value and historical vindication, however, were judged in the light of the covenant tradition.

During and after the exile prophecy took on a new role to exhort and comfort Israel amid the tragedy of its experience. The promises of a renewal of the covenant, and of a new beginning for the people of Yahweh, now had a new and very significant meaning. Whilst others were collecting, considering and revising the ancient traditions of Israel's faith, the prophets still had a part to play in urging the survivors of Israel to launch out afresh in the sure belief that Yahweh had called them to receive the ancient promises. It was as the heralds of a new election that such prophets appeared. Throughout the post-exilic era, and until the time of the destruction of the temple in AD 70, such prophetic hopes of a new coming of Yahweh to Israel to bring in a new experience of salvation, continued to sustain Jewish life. The predictions of a new age of blessing for Israel and of a new, supernatural order of life never lost their power to encourage and strengthen Jewish faith. Such prophecies also rightly gained a place for themselves in Israel's sacred writings, because of their unique witness to the purpose of Yahweh in his covenant with Israel.

The prophets, therefore, only reveal their significance to us when we understand them in the light of the wider history and traditions of Yahwism, which they shared. They neither created a new religion, nor introduced a new morality. To regard their achievement primarily as the introduction of ethical monotheism is to see them out of relation to their religious heritage.[1] The world-sovereignty of Yahweh was already a firmly established idea in Israelite belief long before the time of Amos, as recent investigations into the early Jerusalem cultus have shown. It is misleading in fact to speak of a 'prophetic religion' at all, since such a phrase gives the impression that the prophets either created such a religion, or enjoyed a peculiarly unique experience of religion, which separated them from their environment and heritage in a radical way. The religion of the prophets is the religion of Israel, and the unique contribution which they made was to have interpreted the idea of the covenant at a time when it had fallen into neglect and abuse. Without the prior fact of the covenant the prophets would not be intelligible to us, whilst at the same time it is doubtful whether we should today know anything of what that covenant once meant, were it not for the preaching of such men as Amos and Hosea.

At the beginning of our study we drew attention to two facts that have become important in recent discussion of the nature of an Old Testament theology. The first is that a theology of the Old Testament is not co-terminous with the theological ideas which were actually held by Israelites in the world of Ancient Israel. The latter ideas were inevitably of a much wider and more diverse character than the very limited and selective range of such ideas testified in the Old Testament. The second important fact is that this selective nature of the Old Testament writings is particularly exemplified in the case of the prophets. Prophecy as a whole was not limited to those figures whose writings have been preserved in the Old Testament canon. The recent interest in the place of the cultic prophet in Ancient Israel has therefore attracted fresh interest to a fact that has always been recognized. Its importance, however, has been to show that we have no warrant for assuming that all such prophecy was on a rather low spiritual level. The influence of such cultic prophets on the Psalter belies this glib assessment. And also it over-simplifies the diverse character of

[1] For a criticism of using 'ethical monotheism' as a catchphrase by which to interpret the prophets compare E. Sjöberg, 'De förexiliska profeternas förkunnelse. Några synpunkter', *SEA* 14, 1949, pp. 7ff., and I. Engnell, 'Profetia och tradition. Några synpunkter på ett gammaltestamentligt centralproblem', *SEA* 12, 1947, p. 95.

Israel's religious life and history to assume that such cultic prophets became the 'false' prophets whom we encounter especially
in Micah and Jeremiah. Very probably some of the 'false' prophets
were official representatives of the cult, but they were not all
necessarily so, and neither were all cult-prophets false. The false-
ness of a prophetic oracle could only be detected by its lack of
conformity to historical events,[1] or to the Yahwistic tradition,[2] or
to a genuine prophetic oracle.[3]

This variety in the nature of prophecy in Ancient Israel has
been too easily over-simplified, most particularly by identifying
the cultic prophets as preachers of 'salvation', and the pre-exilic
canonical prophets as preachers of 'woe'. This contrast requires
modification, since, although the cultic prophets sought the
general welfare of Israel as a whole, the preaching of salvation and
judgment was within the compass of their activity before the time
of Amos. It was not simply, therefore, that Amos proclaimed
judgment that led to a new departure in prophecy with his appearance, but that the doom which he pronounced entailed the
dissolution of the covenant. Recent efforts at an interpretation of
Amos 7.10–17, in which the prophet declared the nature and
authority of his calling, have shown that Amos regarded himself
as a prophet like others who had preceded him. He claimed a like
authority to theirs, and he regarded their preaching of judgment
as being similar to his own.[4]

Wherein then lay the distinctiveness of the canonical prophets?
We have sought to show throughout this study that it lay in their
particular relationship to, and concern with, the covenant between
Yahweh and Israel. Their preaching was felt to bear a unique
quality as a witness to what that covenant meant both by way of
demand upon Israel, in the realm of morality, and also by way of
promise for the future. The emphasis of the pre-exilic prophets
upon the judgment of Yahweh on Israel and Judah was felt to be
both morally and spiritually justified, and historically vindicated
by the defeats and exile of 721 and 587 BC. Who the traditionists
were to whom we owe the writing down and preservation of these

[1] Cf. Deut. 18.22.
[2] Cf. Deut. 13.1–5.
[3] Cf. the experience of Jeremiah as recorded in Jer. 28.
[4] Amos 2.11–12; 3.7.

prophetic utterances we shall never know, but they too played their part in Israel's story. It is only by an ultimate reference to the work of the Holy Spirit, who both inspired the prophets and guided these traditionists to cherish their message, that we can explain the canonical status of the prophetic writings. We can, however, point out certain important features which were relevant to Israel's estimate of the canonical prophets. They were believed to have represented the authentic voice of the covenant tradition in the time of its fragmentation and decay. Their moral and spiritual power had a self-authenticating authority to those who were not lacking in spiritual perception. Further, the events of history, in which the whole national life of Israel in both Northern and Southern Kingdoms suffered disaster and collapse, would have been meaningless tragedies if the voices of these prophets had not shown this to be the righteous purpose of God.

It has been a constructive advance in modern study of the prophets to shift the emphasis of research from the prophetic figures themselves, and the psychology of their inspiration, to their message, and the forms of its delivery. We have argued that this message was seen to bear a distinctive witness to the covenant, and that this fact was the primary consideration in its preservation and eventual canonical status. This was not simply because it described the fact of the covenant, or preserved the historical traditions about it, but because it gave a vitally important and elevated interpretation of what that covenant entailed. These prophetic writings, therefore, held a normative, and not merely a descriptive place in Israel's religious traditions. They formed a corpus of writings which raised the level of understanding of Israel as the people of Yahweh to a new height. They were not simply examples of what prophecy had once meant to Israel, but formed a normative standard by which all prophecy, and indeed all Israelite religion, could be tested and understood. The period of history which saw the golden age of the prophets had at its centre the immense crisis of the exile, which placed in jeopardy the entire life and faith of Israel. The prophetic interpretation of this disaster, and the promise of a renewal of divine grace, gave to Israel a spiritual insight which made it possible to accept this defeat and suffering as the will of Yahweh, and to rise from it purified and spiritually strengthened. Behind the preaching of all the canonical prophets we discern the awareness of great events which were changing the whole face of the Near East. Such political and social upheavals inevitably involved Israel and Judah, drawing this divided covenant people into the net of the mighty empires of Assyria, Babylon and Persia. The prophets appeared as Yahweh's messengers to pass on to their people the words which they themselves had received from Yahweh. They were heralds of doom, and yet just because they made this doom intelligible, they became messengers of hope. They foretold and explained what God was doing in their world, showing to Israel the way that Yahweh had laid open for their future. By the light of the covenant, which they knew from the ancient traditions of their people, and through the God of the covenant whom they knew in their own experience, they interpreted the history of their times to those who had to experience its hopes and tragedies.

INDEX OF NAMES

INDEX OF REFERENCES